Matched

KAREN WEINSTOCK

Producer & International Distributor
eBookPro Publishing
www.ebook-pro.com

Matched: From Dating Disasters to Dream Relationships
Karen Weinstock

Contact: relationshipkaren@gmail.com
Website: www.matchedthebook.com

ISBN 9798684941146

To my daughter, Eden, whose light shines so bright, and for whose love and enthusiasm I am so thankful;

To my mother, Bella, who taught me by example how to be a strong, confident, and independent woman;

To my father, Joseph, who taught me that a strong man does not have to be intimidated by a strong woman;

To my family members who have showered me with love;

To Yelena, my comrade in dating and other things—thank you for your friendship, support, and advice;

To my best man, my partner in fun, growth, and love.

Matched

FROM DATING DISASTERS
TO DREAM RELATIONSHIPS

KAREN WEINSTOCK

CONTENTS

ABOUT THE AUTHOR

Karen Weinstock is a top entrepreneurial lawyer. Born in Israel, she served in an elite military unit for two years, then went on to study at the Hebrew University of Jerusalem, ranked in the top 100 universities in the world alongside Harvard, Yale, and Cambridge.

After receiving numerous prestigious job offers at graduation, Karen declined them all—she wanted something more. With no clear roadmap, she immigrated to the United States with two suitcases and a dream. She worked for various law firms but decided she was better suited for entrepreneurship.

Since then, Karen has founded one of the top immigration law firms in the southern United States. Through hard work, grit, and a phenomenal team, her firm has helped thousands of people find their own American dream.

Karen built her multi-million-dollar business—a feat fewer than 1% of women achieve—by mastering sales, marketing, and building relationships and systems. They were skills she would ultimately need in a much greater challenge: finding a lasting and meaningful relationship.

During her marriage, Karen was fulfilled by her career and her role as a mother to an amazing daughter but was unhappy as a wife. She recognized she wanted much more than her partner gave her, and inevitably, resentment grew. Still, Karen believed in marriage, perseverance, and hard work, and she invested many years into working on her relationship, including marriage counseling and reading dozens of relationship books. Ultimately, the truth was undeniable: she and her partner were hopelessly incompatible, and her fourteen-year marriage ended in divorce.

Thus began Karen's journey to find love again—a deep personal search for a meaningful relationship with a romantic and compatible match.

To her dismay, Karen found dating online to be a minefield of inauthenticity and disappointment. Surprisingly, the state of dating advice seemed even more lacking. Wanting to get the most out of dating, and waste less time, effort, and energy on unsuitable partners, she turned to her own skills and background. Combining psychology, the tools and systems she learned growing her business, and the insights of many years of marriage counseling, Karen developed her own unique and easy-to-use system to attract perfect matches.

One of Karen's life missions is to make a difference in the world. Her motivation is to empower both women and men to explore, make good choices, and find meaningful, fulfilling long-term relationships.

INTRODUCTION

The Problem with Chemistry

Picture this:

A man sees an attractive woman in a bar. He approaches, buys her a drink, and they both feel something—a kind of *chemistry*. From there, there's a first date. Then a second, and more chemistry. Before long, a full romance blossoms, complete with all the stomach-fluttering emotions and passionate promises that signify a bright future together.

It's a story we love to tell—a compelling fairytale of magical meetings and instant attraction, where the seeds of a deep, primal connection are planted.

The modern version of this story isn't so different—but this time, the first seeds are planted via a dating app, where we feel many of the same emotional sensations through late-night messages, exchanged photos, and intimate chats. *It's true love,* we think. *Fate.*

The problem with both stories, of course, is that they're not true.

Despite how much we love the feeling of new relationships, chemistry is a poor predictor of compatibility for the long term. That chemistry we so often pin our hopes on isn't so much a formula for happiness as it is a recipe for disaster.

Still, we can't seem to shake the allure of the whirlwind romance.

We love the instant attraction, the passionate connection. *If only I could find that chemistry*, we think, *everything else would be easy.*

But reality tells a different story.

I know this all too well. My relationship with my former husband began with friendship. But as we spent more time together, things began to shift. I was a woman far from home, struggling to find her way, and the attention he gave me felt good. Eventually, I welcomed his physical advances, too—in part because I was lonely and insecure, but also because I realized I had come to feel for him as well. It was chemistry at work.

It would be years before I learned—the hard way—that chemistry doesn't mean compatibility. The powerful attraction and longing we feel in a new romance aren't signs of a bright future, but the effects of a potent cocktail of biological signals called "love hormones" that we enjoy so much that our brains ignore the red flags that normally help us make good decisions. High on dopamine, oxytocin, and other feel-good biological signals, we let ourselves go with wild abandon, despite any and all warning signs. The more our hormones ramp up, the further our IQ seems to plummet in the opposite direction. We lose our ability to plan for the long term and become blind to pitfalls and problems.

The challenge, of course, is that chemistry is wired into us. It's everywhere that people are. It's why so many romantic relationships start in colleges, workplaces, and neighborhoods; those are the places where people frequently come in contact with other people. With time and frequent mixing, we're like the molecules of a chemical mix, interacting and reacting. And once the chemical process starts, it makes no difference whether the love cocktail was mixed during long hours at the office, or during a fleeting moment in a bar. Either way, the outcome is the same: when chemistry floods our brain, we are effectively blind.

What's worse, we now crave the feelings and chase our next "fix" by spending more and more time together trying to recreate them, or by quickly moving on to the next new relationship in an effort to trigger the same sensations. The result is a roller-coaster series of infatuations that cause us to miss out on real love, which comes over time through profound intimacy and experiences.

The chemistry of my marriage broke down slowly, but its lingering effects left me disconnected from my intuition. Instead of trusting my gut and breaking things off, I stayed with my ex, over-analyzing and making excuses. It would be years before I was finally divorced and ready to try again.

This time, however, I was determined not to make the same mistakes.

The Reason Your Relationship Failed

Ask anyone why their last relationship failed, or why their most recent string of dates just hasn't led to anything yet. The most common reason you'll hear is some variation of *they just weren't the right person.*

At its core, this book is about changing that perspective.

The problem with your last relationship wasn't just that you picked the wrong person—although you almost certainly did. But that's not the *cause.* The real problem is that you used the wrong *process* to choose a partner, and it led you to prospects that were never going to work out. Instead of starting with a clear idea of your own needs and wants and a plan for how to satisfy them, you started with chemistry. Like so many of us—including me—you began with that fairytale story of instant connection followed by a "happily ever after" that we long to hear and tell.

In the online world of dating apps, the chemistry problem is compounded. Why? Simply because there is anonymity and millions of potential partners to filter. Each dopamine hit of a new match or a private message triggers the same ancient chemistry. Before we even realize it, we're off and running, telling ourselves that same chemical fairytale.

But chemistry is short-lived. It's about moments, not years. And that makes it not just a terrible way to find a partner, but a dangerous one, too—one that leads to emotional struggle, painful breakups, lost years, and financial loss.

So what's the alternative? That's what this book is about.

Dating Disasters

Israel, where I grew up, is very small. In my community, everyone was into everyone else's business. The upside of the lack of privacy, however, was that it was quite safe for me to date. With a quick phone call or two, I could learn almost anything about my potential dates, like who their parents were, where they grew up, or which schools they had attended. Within minutes, I would know whether a guy was truly decent, a total douchebag, or something in between. A little more digging would usually unearth any skeletons in his closet as well. Had he cheated on his wife? Did he make his child support payments? In Israel, dating held few surprises.

After my divorce, I wanted to find love again. I wanted a deep and meaningful relationship that would last for the rest of my life. Hesitantly, I began to date.

At first, I did what fit with my Israeli roots. I connected through personal acquaintances. Through them, I was slowly connected to singles in our shared network. I was introduced and "fixed up." I went on blind dates and surprise social "arrangements." They were all well-meaning, but the results were always the same: boring first dates, bad matches, and lousy prospects.

Eventually, I pushed myself to start dating online and reluctantly put my profile on a couple of dating apps.

That was when I truly discovered what "Dating 2.0" looked like.

Compared to Israel, the U.S. is huge and largely anonymous. I was shocked to discover that the hot and shirtless Ben Affleck lookalike I met online might really be a 300-pound sloth slobbering on his mother's basement couch. Worse, he might live on another continent altogether, and his end game wasn't a hookup, but simply *a fraud*—a ploy to get women to send money for any one of a number of chemistry-leveraging stories: his (fake) daughter's life-saving medical treatment, a (fake) plane ticket to visit for a romantic weekend, or his (also fake) shipment of diamonds held up in Nigerian customs.

This is no easy maze to navigate. Most relationships now start online through dating apps like Tinder or Bumble. And while dating can *seem* easier—after all, it can be hard to go out in public to meet someone—the tradeoff becomes obvious as soon as you post your profile. It's easy for *anyone*. Now anyone can get in the game for any reason. And not all those reasons are good.

Online dating companies do little to prevent their users from creating fake profiles. Moreover, even if the people you meet online are who they say they are, many of them hide their authentic personality. There are obvious reasons for this, like sex and money. But there are also less tangible ones, like low self-confidence, self-aggrandizing, affirmation, or a need for validation. Some people intentionally mislead; others may do it subconsciously. But whether they're aware of their motives or not, there are good reasons for you to be skeptical of the man who writes he "wants a long-term relationship" or to "find his soul mate."

Despite my best intentions, my luck online was no better than it had been offline. If anything, it was *worse*. Now I was not only dealing with the same issues as before, but they were multiplied by all the added complications of online anonymity. It was a disaster. I made many mistakes, and ultimately wasted a tremendous amount of time on unsuitable partners. Eventually, I'd had enough.

I'm a lawyer, I thought. *I'm a successful entrepreneur. I graduated from a top university. I served in an elite military unit! Why can't I figure out dating, of all things?*

It was time for a different approach.

The Real Problem with Dating

My quest began with books about online dating, which offered a little insight but didn't hold much promise to solve my real problem. Still, I took what made sense and added it to my growing understanding of why dating failed or succeeded.

By this point, I was also a veteran of many years of marriage counseling and the avid reader of dozens of books on relationships and psychology. They didn't contain the "secret sauce" for dating either, but they helped me gain some useful insights about long-term relationships.

It was then that I turned my attention to my business. I had over two decades of experience in marketing, sales, interviewing applicants for positions, and building relationships with colleagues and clients. What's more, I was good at it. Dating, I realized, had many similarities to job searching, interviewing, and sales. Building a successful business is all about long-term relationships; not only was that exactly what I wanted, but also, I was good at it!

That's when the light bulb came on. I had no trouble finding men online—the challenge was finding the *right* ones. After making almost every dating mistake imaginable, I had reached the root of the problem. By the time I was on a date, the mistake had already been made. By then, I'd wasted my time and energy on someone that was never a match, to begin with.

Instead, I realized, I needed a way to attract and screen potential partners long before I ever even *messaged* them, never mind met them in person.

I needed a system.

Matched: Moving from Chemistry to Clarity

In many cultures, relationships are predicated on whether the other person is from a good family or has a good career or career potential. Or, if we want to get into stereotypes, men generally seek beauty, youth, and sex, whereas women value men's companionship, loyalty, success, and status.

Times have changed, however, and many of our old ways of screening are no longer enough to deal with the new world of online dating, or the new roles and aspirations of those who date.

I've developed a successful system to bridge that gap. It can help you not only circumvent the shady characters and other risks of online dating, but it can show you how to find meaningful relationships with the *real* people who are most likely to be compatible with you. You *can* have fun on your dates, enjoy who you're meeting, and get to know like-minded people who can be your friends as well as potential long-term partners. Using my system, you can cut through the masks, the lies, and the bullshit fast, and find a fulfilling, long-term relationship with someone with whom you share a mutual love, based on who each of you *really* are.

Successful dating is about avoiding issues before they happen. It's about screening out the people who don't fit *before* chemistry has a chance to confuse things. Most people do not really stop to think about what they are actually looking for in a partner or a relationship. Using the approach in the pages that follow, I learned to quickly and easily know whether someone would (or would not) be a good match for me. I reached a point where I could eliminate most men in a matter of seconds, some in minutes, and even the higher quality ones after only an hour or two. Only a select few make it to a first date, far less to the second date, and most of my second dates eventually turned into good relationships.

Your Path from Dating Disasters to Dream Relationships

After countless trials, almost as many mistakes, and an obsessive drive to figure out what works and what doesn't, I developed the three-step system that makes up this book:

1. *Preparation.* This first step will take some time to complete, but it is well worth the investment of time and effort to do it well. Every hour you invest in getting to understand yourself and your needs will save you days, months, and years of frustration and agony in the future.

2. *Screening.* This step will help you filter out only those who are a good potential match for the "you" that you've revealed in step one. You'll learn to quickly and comfortably exclude the matches

that waste your time, confuse your chemistry, and lead you to miss those who are a good fit.

3. *Dating.* Finally, you'll learn how to successfully navigate the transition to the real world of in-person dating, avoiding the most common pitfalls and risks, and learning to assess people as they are, not as they pretend to be. When you determine your partner is a good potential match, you'll use practical tools to help grow your new relationship into your dream one.

Not all your dates will be a success. There are many variables, including chemistry, that do indeed have an important role to play. But the goal isn't to find the right person on day one—it's to exclude more of the *wrong* ones so that you can spend more time with those that are a better fit for everything that is unique about *you.*

As I improved my system over time, my dating improved exponentially. Eventually, almost everyone I dated was a great person, and a great potential match based on my (very picky) criteria. Some of my dates would become good friends, while others blossomed into long-term, loving relationships. In all cases, I had managed to avoid the drama, risk, and disappointment that was so common in the dating world.

My goal was never to "win" at the game of dating. I wanted to save time and cut through the bullshit. I wanted to win at *future* relationships—to give the gift of a lasting, quality romantic relationship to my future self. And that's the same thing I want for you. To learn more about how *you* can be successful at dating and find your dream relationship, read on!

CHAPTER 1

Find Your "Why"

Achievement happens when we pursue and attain what we want. Success comes when we are in clear pursuit of why we want it.

-Simon Sinek

In Simon Sinek's brilliant and engaging TED Talk, "How Great Leaders Inspire Action," he explains what differentiates the great leaders and companies of the world. If you haven't already, it's well worth taking twenty minutes to watch his talk—his performance is a powerful lesson that explains why your own motivation is so critical to understand *before* you begin your search for a partner. Your *why* is everything, and it needs to come before anything else in your journey to find a lasting relationship.

To find meaningful relationships with people you like, love, and get along with, you have to dig deep and know your *why*. Before setting up your profile, much less going on dates at full speed, you must pause and do the essential groundwork on yourself—starting with finding your *why*. As Sinek says, "People don't buy what you do; they buy why you do it. And what you do simply proves what you believe."

If you know the real reasons why you want a relationship, including who you are, and how your core passions will be aligned, you'll be more motivated, more focused, and you'll enjoy the process of dating much more. Best of all, you'll get a much better outcome!

During my divorce, I fought tirelessly for primary custody of my daughter instead of agreeing to a 50/50 split. It was emotionally exhausting and financially draining, but what kept me going was my powerful *why*: the well-being of my daughter. She has some challenges and needs a lot of structure and loving support. I knew that I was better equipped than my ex to provide what she needed—both short-term and long-term. This strong *why* propelled me through much stress and uncertainty, as well as a two-year court battle, because I believed I was doing the best thing for my daughter. It was a *why* that no obstacle could stop.

In the world of dating, *why* is just as relevant. Most relationship *whys* are universal. Humans are social creatures, and most of us are wired to crave company and thrive among others. (The relatively small minority who isn't, is not reading this book!) Generally, both men and women have strong and common *whys*. First and foremost is our biological need for companionship, touch, and sex, all of which require physical proximity. It may not always be at the forefront of our consciousness, but our drive to survive and continue our species is biologically encoded in our unconscious brain.

Consider that it is usually more fun and satisfying to engage in life *with other people*—to do things like going out to restaurants or movies, or to go traveling. When good things happen to us—for example, we get a promotion at work—we enjoy it far more when we can share our success with a loved one; the shared experience intensifies our positive feelings of pride, happiness, and excitement. Similarly, when we have a bad day, let's say we were fired, having our partner support us is a much-needed comfort. Even having someone simply listen to us has enormous psychological benefits. Companionship is an undeniable social need.

These are universal *whys*. Your task now is to think about your individual motivation. Look inside and ask yourself these questions:

- Why do you want a relationship? Are you just lonely and want sex or companionship?
- Do you want to start a family with kids?
- Have you just broken up and want validation that you still have what it takes?
- Do you want a father or mother to your children because your ex is no longer in the picture?
- Are you under financial strain and want someone who will offer you financial support?
- Do you want a partner to live with you or to marry?
- Are you looking for a "part-time" partner? Do you want to maintain separate households and see each other mainly on weekends and holidays?

Whatever your *why* is—your main reason for dating—you must be brutally honest with yourself if you expect to find someone who matches with that reason. By tapping into your motivations and intentions, you'll become much more focused in your quest.

I have seen the power of this approach many times. My friend Nancy has a unique personality; she is larger than life and the center of attention wherever she goes. She is a people person with the natural ability to make anyone feel at ease, yet, at the same time, she is high-strung, suffers from anxiety, and has extreme emotional reactions to the stresses in her life.

Nancy has two teenage children and receives no financial support from her ex-husband (their father). Since he moved out of state, she has been a true single mom and the sole breadwinner for her household. When I asked her what her *whys* were, she stated the obvious. She wanted to fall in love again and experience life with a man, to enjoy intimacy, to go out to restaurants and movies, to travel, and more.

What Nancy was telling me wasn't her real *why*, and I urged her to dig deeper. "*Why* do you want to enjoy intimacy with a man?" I asked. "What does it *mean* to you?" With enough prompting, it turned out that Nancy was desperate to have a "human Valium"— someone who could calm her down when she became stressed and help to relieve her anxiety. Moreover, she wanted a man that she could depend on financially. And lastly, she wanted someone who could co-parent and who would be a good role model for her teenagers, who often pushed her limits.

In short, Nancy wanted a male to take charge and give her peace and stability, both mentally and financially. None of this was surprising or unreasonable, but it illustrated a point: once she dug deep and realized these things, she had much greater clarity about the kind of man she would want to date. Nancy *thought* she was looking just for fun-activities and restaurant-hopping guy, but she wasn't. Instead, "calm" and "easygoing" became absolutely necessary qualities for her match, and she quickly broke it off with a man she was seeing at the time so that she could search for one who would fit her *why*.

My friend Ellie also found great dating clarity by working to uncover her *why*. She's a high-powered fifty-year-old, who has a very demanding career where she has to travel the world to consult with Fortune 500 companies. Ellie works long hours and is a partner in her business, making over half a million dollars a year. She has more air miles and hotel bonus points than she could ever spend and has been saving them for her retirement. Her only child is in college.

Needless to say, Ellie is used to the finer things in life. Without question, her *why* is companionship. She wanted to have someone to come home to after busy business trips and tours. She wanted someone who would take care of her *physically*, not financially—someone who would be waiting for her with a hot meal and a warm bed when she returned from her travels. She did not want to come home to an empty house, as she so cherished the moments she spent at home versus hotels and airports.

Ellie didn't care how much money her partner made—she already made more than enough. What she wanted was to completely unwind and make herself at home, going from being "all business" during the week to "all pleasure" on the weekend. Armed with this clear insight into her *why*, she soon matched well with a man who was not career-oriented, but was happy to be a "house husband." His personality was ideal for her desires; he was a sweet and loving guy who would dedicate his life to making her happy. He genuinely enjoyed pampering her—delighting her with gifts, romantic walks, and delicious meals.

These are just two examples of the many people who have used a deep look into their dating *why* to find a better match. You can do the same with the following exercise.

Exercise: Find Your Why

List the top five reasons (at least) why you want to get into a relationship. Make sure to take into account your current situation in life (never married, divorced, have children, want children, do not want children, career issues, restraints, etc.)

Be sure to dig deeper into your inner needs and desires than you ever have before; you may be surprised at what you find!

1)
2)
3)
4)
5)

When you have clarity about what motivates you—about what you want and *why*— then you've completed the critical first step. Let's carry on!

CHAPTER 2

Ready (or Not)?

Your task is not to seek for love, but merely to seek and find all the barriers within yourself that you have built against it.

—Rumi

Congratulations—you've found your *why*! Now that you understand your real motivation for dating, the next step in the preparation phase is to examine whether you are truly *ready* to date.

Yes, it is possible to have one without the other. Even with a strong *why* you may simply not be ready. Before you begin to date, you'll need to honestly and thoroughly evaluate whether the time is right. Don't wait for the "perfect" time to date, as it may never come. But, if you aren't ready—for whatever reason—you won't show up well as a potential partner, and you won't attract a quality match or one that can grow into a long-term fulfilling relationship.

Self-awareness isn't easy, but it is possible. The following four questions will help you decide if you're ready.

Question 1: Do I truly *like* myself?

This is the question of all questions, and if the answer is *no*, please stop here and take the time you need to work on yourself until you reach a definitive YES! If you suffer from psychological problems or personal issues, it's critical that you work on yourself first to resolve or improve them—until you do, you'll struggle to attract or keep a high-quality partner.

At the heart of whether you genuinely like yourself is your self-esteem, something that both men and women struggle with, some more than occasionally. Low self-esteem affects every aspect of life, from employment opportunities and social interactions to mental health. Dating is no exception; relationships top the list of things in life negatively affected by poor self-esteem. If you can't answer yes to the question, "Do I truly like myself?" you'll be well served by taking the time to work on yourself.

Women are more likely to have self-esteem and shame issues surrounding their weight and overall appearance, and we tend to invest a lot of time, money, and effort in makeup, hair, nails, clothes, shoes, and accessories. But what drives this? The media plays a huge role, portraying skinny models and flawless (and photoshopped) actresses as the norm. While the average woman in America is 5'4" tall and weighs 170 pounds, the "average" model is 5'10" tall and weighs between 100 and 150 pounds—25% less than the healthy weight recommendation. No *wonder* even us "normal" women suffer from low self-esteem!

Make no mistake: it's essential to take care of yourself, both on the inside and the outside—just be sure to consider your motives. You want to be healthy and present yourself in the best light possible while dating, but remember that good self-esteem can be far more attractive than losing thirty pounds or having plastic surgery. There's nothing wrong with working toward the personal benefits of a healthier lifestyle through nutrition and exercise. But that doesn't mean that you have to wait until you accomplish those goals before you can like yourself.

Consider Jennifer, a brilliant and successful top executive. She wore designer suits, and her makeup, hair, and nails were always meticulous. She carried herself with great poise, and at first glance, particularly in a work setting, she was self-confident.

At home, however, things were starkly different. Her (ex)husband was abusive, both mentally and physically. He knew that she was sensitive about her weight and used that knowledge to attack her confidence. When they were going through a divorce, he called her a cow and told her that no one would ever be attracted to her. Jennifer, for all her confidence at work, was convinced it was true; her self-esteem was destroyed.

When the time came to begin dating, Jennifer still believed her abusive husband's words. She was sure no one would be attracted to her, and so she skipped the step of working on herself—after all, why bother?

As a result, Jennifer clung to the first man who showed her any attention after her divorce. For a fleeting moment, she felt desired, attractive, and perhaps even loved. The trouble was that the man was married and had no intention of leaving his wife. This only added to Jennifer's insecurities. She felt "less than" the man's wife. Her fears were reinforced. Now she was in second place, undesirable and rejected yet again.

When that relationship ended, Jennifer fell right into the arms of the very next man who made her feel attractive. He showered her with compliments and attention but turned out to be a fraud who only wanted her money. It took months for Jennifer to untangle his web of lies, and she ultimately broke it off with him as well. Left with the sense of betrayal and the shame of having not seen through his façade sooner, she felt her confidence take another hit.

By now, Jennifer was becoming aware that she needed to work on herself. Deep down, she knew she deserved better than these men, better than her ex-husband, better than anyone who did not see her beauty and qualities. As Jennifer began to look inside, she realized her lack of self-esteem had led her to settle for whoever gave her a little attention. It was time to rebuild her self-esteem.

Part of her journey included getting back in shape, both inside and out. Jennifer hadn't worked out in years, so she hired a personal trainer. She began to see a therapist who helped her overcome her self-confidence issues and realize what a catch she truly was.

When Jennifer began dating again a few months later, she was a transformed person. This time, her new self-esteem gave her the strength to be far more selective, which became an attractive quality in her as well. Jennifer had realized she could and did feel good about herself *without* the attention of a man; this time, her ability to take her time with no sense of desperation paid off in the form of a quality partner. She met a kind, successful, and genuine man who was attracted to her for all the right reasons, including her newfound confidence.

Yes, it's true that much of our initial attraction to another person is based on looks. But it's just that—an *initial* attraction. While most men can appreciate aesthetic beauty in a woman, the majority are not obsessed with looks alone. And for the ones who are, is someone who is that superficial and self-absorbed really someone you would want as a partner? If so, be prepared for them to be always looking for the next, younger, newer "model". Right or wrong, that's what is most important to them. (More on this in Chapter 4: Your Ideal Partner.)

Question 2: Do I think I *need* a partner to complete me?

Like many women who watched the movie, *Jerry Maguire*, I loved the moment when Tom Cruise said to Renée Zellweger, "You complete me."

Like many women, however, I now cringe when I hear both the line and its subtext that we need a partner to make us whole. If you are under the impression that you are incomplete in any way, or that you *need* someone else to "complete" you, stop right here. As with the goal of genuinely liking yourself, it's time to do some inner work.

Each of us must learn that we *can* live alone and have a fulfilling life as an independent being. That may not be what you desire, but there is power in coming to understand that you will be okay even if you don't find a partner, or if it merely takes time. I learned the hard way that I would rather be alone than with the wrong person. Likewise, I would rather be alone than waste my time on endless first dates that do not lead anywhere worthwhile.

To begin your journey to find out who you really are, start with finding out what makes *you* happy (as opposed to your potential partner), and then *do it*. Do you enjoy painting? Take a class with a friend or even alone. Did you always want a motorcycle, but your previous partner wouldn't "let" you have one? Buy it! Do you enjoy cooking? Spend a day preparing an elaborate meal for a couple of close friends, for you and your child(ren), or just for yourself! Have you always toyed with the idea of going back to school? *Do it!* Is traveling your passion, but you always thought you had to have someone to go with you? Take a road trip alone with no one else's agenda to worry about. You can go when, where, and for however long you want. And, let's be real. Do you need sexual gratification? There are plenty of ways to take care of yourself solo. (Another great benefit of that road trip by yourself!)

In short, quit worrying about the world *outside* you. There is an entire world *within* you—with, or without, a significant other.

I have not forgotten that this book is about "finding your dream relationship," not "learning to live alone forever." We'll begin discussing in detail what you are looking for in a mate in Chapter 4 (Your Ideal Partner). But when you do begin that process, make sure to look for someone with characteristics that *complement* you, rather than someone who you think will somehow *complete* you. You must feel confident that you truly are a complete person as you are right now, and that you are worthy of meaningful connection and love. A quality partner can and will teach you things, encourage you to get outside your comfort zone, and balance you. But you must be convinced that you are complete as you are—with or without someone else.

Question 3: Am I truly *ready* for a relationship?

Asking yourself if you are ready for a relationship means more than, "Do I want one, and want one right now?"

Are you *truly* ready? For example, do you have any baggage from past relationships that you still carry with you? Are you completely—truly *completely*—over your last relationship? Will you bring any preconceived notions or biases into your next? What can you do to avoid this?

We all inevitably have baggage. No one gets through life without a story to tell, and your life experience thus far has shaped who you are today. We cannot, nor should we, forget the past. However, there is a big difference between *learning* from past experiences and *living* in them. Similarly, there is a vast difference between a previous relationship and a current one, even if you have a pattern or are generally attracted to the same "type."

What stories are you still carrying that don't serve you? Are you still bitter about your divorce? Do you think all women are manipulative and vindictive? Do you assume all men are liars and cheats? Are you still mourning your last relationship?

Sarah tolerated a twenty-year marriage, during which her husband constantly lied and cheated. It devastated her, but she put up with it, waiting until the children left home to file for divorce. Not surprisingly, when she began to date again, there were serious trust issues. They bubbled up almost immediately after she met Dave.

Sarah and Dave had a lovely first date, and then a truly amazing second date at a romantic restaurant on the beach. They talked for hours, discussing their kids, their interests, and their jobs. Sarah was relieved to learn that Dave had a stable and successful career; her ex had spent long periods unemployed. At the end of the date, Dave passionately kissed her. For the first time in twenty years, Sarah felt young and alive again.

It took only a few hours for her trust issues to kick in. The very next day, Sarah called Dave's place of work surreptitiously (or so she thought). For Sarah, it seemed innocent enough; she was just confirming for herself that he really worked there and had the position he claimed.

Her Prince Charming saw things differently. When Dave found out, he was so angry and upset that he never wanted to see Sarah again.

While her actions made perfect sense for someone walking in her shoes, her trust issues made her appear less than stable to the man on the other side of them. In the end, Sarah's baggage caused Dave to send her packing.

Sarah didn't need to disregard her concerns completely, but she did need to learn how to cautiously but logically develop trust. There are many quality men and women out there who are honest. Sarah's job was to do the inner work necessary to change her paradigm that all men are liars.

Eventually, Sarah developed a system of "trust but verify"—and verify *discreetly*—which worked well.

Similarly, a rebound relationship inevitably carries baggage and isn't healthy or productive for anyone involved. I developed strong feelings for Collin, a gorgeous blue-eyed and dark-haired professional who appeared wholly smitten with me during our first date. The attraction was mutual, and on the second date, when we kissed, it was magical. I felt butterflies deep in my stomach. The problem was that Collin, who was newly divorced, wasn't ready.

Collin and his ex had lived together as little more than roommates for the last years of their marriage, and he desperately wanted to feel love and intimacy right away. But he had not taken the time to think about what *else* he wanted in a relationship. Furthermore, because the divorce was so new, both for Collin and his children, he was still on a daily emotional roller coaster. Collin worried almost constantly (and understandably) about the effects of the divorce on his children. And even though he was the one who wanted the divorce, he was still going through a period of grieving.

Jumping into a relationship with me (or anyone) was too much, too soon, and ultimately hurtful for both of us. The many issues related to Collin's marriage and divorce meant that he was distracted and emotionally unavailable to give me what I wanted and needed. Simply put, Collin just wasn't *ready*. No matter how great he was, or well-suited we were, it simply wasn't going to work at that point in time—and it didn't. Timing also must be right in addition to the match.

These stories serve to illustrate that being well-matched is no substitute for being *ready*. No matter what the reason, if you are not ready for a relationship, you need to work on *yourself*, first and foremost.

To be clear, that doesn't mean you have to be *alone*. You certainly could consider a casual relationship, companionship, or even a "friends with benefits" arrangement that may work for you in the interim. The important thing is that you continue to work on yourself before trying to find a long-term match.

Question 4: Is my *mind* in the right place?

Think about the times you have decided to diet and exercise in preparation for a trip, a wedding, or a class reunion. We want to get our body "right" before putting it out there. Yet we often fail to give the same attention to our *minds*—a far *more* important objective. Only when you get your mind "right" will you be able to attract the right kind of partner, and ultimately enjoy a lasting and meaningful relationship.

Dating can be a roller coaster, and it is critical to set up the right mental attitude before you start. You must believe that you are worthy of a quality partner and that he or she is out there; only then will you be able to find and attract him or her.

There is more to this than liking yourself. You need to also believe in *abundance*. There is plenty of fish in the sea (pun intended for you online dating aficionados, although I never tried the *Plen-tyofFish* dating app myself). There are plenty of quality partners out there who are interested in you. Your job is to find the ones in whom *you* are also interested.

Many people believe in scarcity instead and bemoan their limited resources. For them, there is never enough money, time, prospects, or potential. I choose to believe that time is the only truly limited resource we have; there really are only twenty-four hours in each day, seven days in a week—no less, and no more. Therefore, I choose to spend my time wisely and manage it instead of it managing me. It's why I created a better approach to dating. I wanted a quick way to weed through all the bullshit and get to *quality* connections. Part of that process requires that you believe—that you know with *certainty*—that there is an abundance of partners for you out there, and an abundance of love, too. We all have abundant love to give to others, and we all are worthy of receiving it in return.

Now that you have found your *why*, have the right mental attitude, and have decided that you are genuinely ready for a relationship, read on! It's time to begin the process of transforming thoughts into actions and opening the door to a fulfilling dating experience.

CHAPTER 3

Search Within

Look well into thyself; there is a source that will always spring up if thou wilt always search there.

— Marcus Aurelius

Congratulations on deciding that you are indeed ready to find your next relationship! I know firsthand how difficult it can be and how much strength it can take. Before you go any further, take a few moments to appreciate how far you've already come.

Before you launch into the exciting step of choosing your ideal partner in the next chapter, we're going to take one more critical look at *you.*

You've found your *why* and are certain that you are ready. Now it's time to take a look at your own mental and emotional mirror using five critical questions that you must answer before taking the next step.

Preparation Pays Off

Anna thought she was ready to re-enter the dating world and finally had a first date. Both excited and nervous, she put tremendous effort into her makeup, hair, and clothing. Although it was just a coffee date, Anna went so far as to consult her teenage daughter for fashion advice to ensure she made a good first impression. She even tried to decide in advance what to talk about and what funny things she might say. By most standards, Anna was a model of preparation.

Sure enough, things began with a great conversation about their jobs and interests. Then, out of the blue, her date abruptly said he had to go. He didn't even let her finish her coffee before leaving with barely a goodbye.

Humiliated, Anna walked out of the café, crawled into her car, and simply cried. She had no idea what she had done wrong, why her date hadn't liked her, and why he seemed to literally get up and run.

When Anna confided in me, she mentioned that her date had done most of the talking—about himself, it seemed—and in retrospect, she realized he was probably quite self-absorbed. Based on the behavior she described, I agreed with her analysis, and comforted her that it was perhaps better they had not hit it off; she, like all of us, needed someone who cared about her, too.

Anna, however, was still unsettled by the experience and could not resist the urge to text him to ask why he had left so abruptly. He responded simply: *Not my type.*

The blunt reply was painful at first, but with time, Anna began to see that this was the real source of the problem. She *wasn't* his type—and he wasn't hers! They were simply not well matched.

But what *was* a good match? She'd invested hours preparing for the date, but none of that preparation was focused on her inside world. She'd done no introspection. She had no way to tell who was a match. She realized because she didn't know *herself* well enough, let alone what kind of person she wanted.

Before her next date, Anna invested time in *substantial* internal preparation and got significantly better results. Her date would have been well-served had he done the same! She didn't neglect her physical appearance, but that mattered far less, she realized, than understanding herself *first* so that she could identify what she wanted.

This preparation is vital. Thinking first about your *why* (Chapter 1), who you are (Chapters 2 and 3), and then who and what you want (Chapters 4 and 5), allows you to search for and market to your ideal mate. You can then confidently venture out into the dating sphere and get better results in less time.

Far too many people skip some or even all of these critical preparation steps and, therefore, waste time chasing a poor match. They end up with dates or even partners with whom they are entirely incompatible, and who they never really wanted in the first place. Sooner or later, every bad match has a bad ending. Preventing that starts with good preparation.

The Five Questions

Before you go any further, it's time to think about who you *really* are. Who are you at your core? What kind of people, activities, and things do you enjoy? What are your deal-breakers in a relationship? Who and what inspires you? What irritates you? What makes you get out of bed in the morning? What are your dislikes, or even your *hates*? What are your passions?

The following five questions will help you find out. After reading each one, stop reading, close your eyes, and simply think about the questions for fifteen minutes. Or thirty. Or even more. Take as long as you need! Get a glass of wine, light some candles, and put on some nice music; it's time to find out who you really are.

Question 1: What are my best attributes?

We can all be defined both by our best and worst attributes. When it comes to dating apps, however, you want to focus on your positive aspects without being deceptive. There's no value in scaring away potential suitors right off the bat.

To begin, list ten attributes or characteristics that uniquely describe you:

1)
2)
3)
4)
5)
6)
7)
8)
9)
10)

If you feel stuck, ask friends and family about your personality to get ideas or to validate your choices. Simply tell them: *I'm doing an exercise about what is special and unique about me and what I have to offer to a friend or companion. Please let me know your honest thoughts.* Write down their responses. In large part, their answers should match what you wrote, although people may see you differently than how you view yourself.

Here's a short list of what my friends generated for me: *fun, creative, happy, powerful, driven, go-getter, loyal, great mother, talented, ambitious, musical, good friend, brilliant, good listener, focused, motivated, tenacious, extraordinary, entrepreneurial, influential, strong-willed,* and *amazing.*

Not only did they help fill out my list, but the descriptions filled up my confidence, too! Now all I had to do was narrow the list down to the top ten that I thought would work best for dating. In the end, I dropped *strong-willed* even though it is very true!

If there's a significant gap between how your friends describe you and how you see yourself, take the time to self-reflect; if you are honest with yourself and others, there shouldn't be much difference. If the difference is vast, then you need to examine why your results are what they are. Either you are not putting forward a genuine version of yourself, you're too hard on yourself, or those around you don't understand you well.

If you still need help, we have compiled a research-backed list that you can use to find qualities that resonate the most with you – it is available under resources at the end of the book. Once you've identified those, narrow the list down to your top ten.

Why is this so important? Consciously or subconsciously, we look for and are most compatible with people who share at least some of the same attributes as us. For example, I know that I have above-average intelligence, and I am looking for the same thing in a man. That may seem vain, but it's not—it's an effort to get *real.* Honesty is in short supply in the world of dating and finding it starts with you. You don't have to display your answers for the world to see, but if you look inside, you'll find you already know many "yes" or "no" attributes in a partner. You might never be compatible with someone who is too messy, for example, or someone whose employment is not consistent because these are just too different from your own characteristics.

Similarly, a man with average intelligence is just not enough for me in a partner. I was briefly in such a situation, and it didn't last long. The man did not challenge me and had nothing to teach me. But when my brain sparks with another person on an intellectually-level playing field, I form a deeper and more meaningful connection and stay engaged longer. I'm not ashamed to admit that I would be bored silly in a relationship where I was significantly smarter than my partner. Likewise, you shouldn't be embarrassed to define your attributes and seek out others who have the ones you value.

Since no one will be reading your list, be absolutely truthful, even if you know that some of your attributes may not be considered positive or pleasant by everyone. For example, I am well aware that I am high-maintenance in some areas, whereas in others, I am easygoing and fun. I'm happy to let my date choose the restaurant, for example, but I can admit that I need my partner's complete attention, energy, and focus, at least when we are together without kids and work. I don't want to spend a vacation at the Motel 6, but I don't necessarily expect the Ritz, either. (Other than my birthday, an anniversary, or other special occasions. Okay, fine. I want at least a *little* Ritz. I prefer to stay in nice accommodations, and I'm perfectly willing to pay for it.)

Not all these qualities are ones that you'll place front and center in a dating profile. I wouldn't state that I am high-maintenance, because it's not endearing or entirely true, nor would I list that I am easygoing, as this isn't entirely true either. Being untruthful is a recipe for disaster later on. It would be a huge surprise for a partner, for instance, when I declined to spend a romantic weekend at his cousin's cabin in the woods with no indoor plumbing. And it wouldn't last, even if there was initial chemistry.

Question 2: What are my core values?

My client Nate had immigrated to the U.S. from an impoverished country and then done extremely well for himself financially. After completing his medical residency here with a specialization in general surgery, Nate began to send a large portion of his net income back home—not just to family members, but to non-profit organizations like orphanages, and to individuals that he learned were struggling or suffering.

Nate began dating a woman, Lillian, who had also grown up in poverty. Lillian was no gold-digger; she was educated and had a thriving career of her own as an architect. But unlike Nate, Lillian's background and later financial success did not lead to her wanting to give back. In fact, it was the direct opposite. Lillian's mantras were more like, "You only live once," and, "You can't take it with you!" She chose to spend every dollar she made, and that spending never included anything charitable.

As Nate and Lillian grew closer and began to share their financial situations, Lillian was horrified to learn that Nate would "give away" so much of his money, and began to criticize him. Conversely, Nate was horrified to learn that Lillian "did not give a damn" (as he put it) about anyone but herself. Eventually, it ended their relationship.

What drove Nate and Lillian apart was a fundamental difference in *values*. Some of Nate's top core values were compassion and generosity, and that influenced how he spent his money. Lillian valued personal enjoyment and living in the moment, and that affected her spending, too. In the end, that critical difference in values was insurmountable.

By definition, values are what we find most important. Along with your attributes and characteristics, values are what define you and make you unique. Understanding yours will not only make you more self-aware but will form an excellent screening mechanism for potential partners. If a date does not share your values or has diametrically opposed ones, there's no need to go any further.

To get started, get out your pencil again (or a Sharpie) and list the top ten values that you hold nearest and dearest:

1)

2)

3)

4)

5)

6)

7)

8)

9)

10)

If you're stuck, use the helpful values list at the resources section, and narrow the values listed there to your top ten.

What values do you cherish? For me, integrity and excellence are high on the list, as is personal growth. Consequently, if a guy can't keep his word or isn't curious and growth-oriented, we won't mesh well.

Family is also one of my top values, so spending quality time with my daughter and being the best mother I can be are extremely important. A partner who doesn't understand that would not last long. I am also interested in deep, meaningful relationships—not the shallow type. I appreciate getting to know someone, including all their weird habits and imperfections—and them getting to know mine as well! As a result, the superficial type would never match well with me.

Question 3: What are my core beliefs?

While your values define what you hold most important, your beliefs describe what you hold to be *true*.

For example, you and a potential partner might hold religious faith as a core value. But *which* faith? If his beliefs are deeply rooted in Christianity, and yours in Buddhism, that shared value of faith is not going to get you far. The high value you both place in faith, but with opposite beliefs, would most likely be the death of a relationship in the long run.

If you both value "love" or "fidelity," but your beliefs embrace homosexuality, and his do not, you're going to face challenges. Likewise, if you both value love, but you believe in absolute monogamy and he in polyamory, you're going to have conflict. Similar values do not necessarily equate with similar beliefs.

What core beliefs do you have about life, spirituality, and relationships? Do you believe in marriage to one person for life? Or do you believe you are here to experience as many relationships as possible? Do you think both men and women are equal in a relationship, or do you believe that the man needs to be the leader and provider? Do you believe that we all will spend eternity in heaven or hell, or do you think life's a bitch and then you die?

If you're like many people, you've never considered your beliefs in detail, particularly in the context of dating. Now's your chance! *My core beliefs about life, spirituality, and relationships are:*

1)

2)

3)

4)

5)

6)

7)

8)

9)

10)

It's critical that you disclose your faith—or absence thereof—and its intensity in your profile, or in "getting to know you" conversations with a potential partner.

Your strong beliefs (which are intertwined with your faith and values) are *the* single most crucial thing to reflect on and be completely honest about on your profile. Whether you are a devout Catholic or an Atheist, a Buddhist or Agnostic, you must share your beliefs upfront. While you can certainly be close friends with people of different faiths, a romantic relationship is a different thing altogether.

You should also be as forthcoming as possible about your gender, your sexual preference, and if you have children—particularly if those things are connected to your faith. Do not hold your strong beliefs back for later disclosure, for any reason. If faith is not a deal-breaker for either of you, it is more than possible to work

around religious differences simply because they aren't as important to you. Likewise, some people actually convert to a different
faith, or become less or more observant of their faith, to match their
partner's needs. I have a Japanese friend who converted to Judaism
to marry an Orthodox Jewish man she loved. For her, faith was not
a point of contention—what mattered was the relationship.

You should be prepared and open to discussing faith and your
strong beliefs right out of the gate. This should weed out incompatible suitors and relationships that would be doomed to fail.

To do that, however, you must be willing to reflect on whether
faith is essential to you and be able to articulate what it is that you
value so much about it. Many people list "Agnostic" on their profile
because they genuinely are. But others do it because they simply
don't care about religion at all. Whatever your reasons, be clear.
Share your religion (or lack thereof), but also how devout you are
(or are not). If you are devout in your faith, do you require the same
from your partner? A conflict of faith can be cataclysmic in a relationship—the time to avoid such a situation for both of you is *early*.

Differences in faith and religion often come to light in partners
with young children who conflict in how to raise them and what
beliefs and values they want to instill. Again, these things need to
be discussed early on if there is potential chemistry. It's far better
for everyone to address this before someone gets hurt.

I was born Jewish, and while I believe in many Christian values,
I am not Christian. If I date someone who is a devout Christian
and expects me to get baptized, we won't match as a couple, plain
and simple. Conversely, I may be open to having a Christmas tree
at home if it's a must for a man I love. (I would, however, have to
give thought to the potential conflict since I fully intend to raise my
daughter as a Jew, and to preserve our family's faith, traditions, and

values.) There's no right answer for everyone—only a right answer for *me*. What matters is that I carefully consider faith in the context of dating.

That being said, I list my religious belief on my profile as "other." There are a couple of reasons for this. The first is that spirituality is more important to me than organized religion and the strict rules and dogma that go with it. I once had a wonderful relationship with a man who was born a Hindu, but like me, was more spiritual than religious. We each respected our individual beliefs and choices—the kind of symbiosis you should seek if you and a partner are of a different faith.

The second reason I list "other" on my profile is that there are very few available Jewish men where I live, and even fewer who I am attracted to. I felt it would severely limit my pool of potential matches if I listed my religion on my profile.

In my case, Jewish men who saw my profile were able to assume I was Jewish because I listed that I speak Hebrew. Many Jewish men would then start a conversation with me because it was rare for them to find a single Jewish woman dating online.

For my part, whenever I encountered men who listed faith as being "very important" to them (even if it was Judaism), I did not initiate a conversation with them at all. I felt the odds of a potential beliefs-based problem with a highly devout partner (regardless of faith) outweighed the benefits.

One day, I started a conversation on an app with a man who piqued my interest and had an interesting profile. I found it curious that he didn't have children and had never been married, despite being in his mid-forties, and I felt it was important to ask him why. After exchanging a few pleasantries, here is how the conversation went:

Karen: *So, you've never been married?*

Gordon: *Was engaged once. Would have to be 110% sure. I do not believe in divorce.*

Karen: *So faith is important to you?*

Gordon: *Extremely. Staunch Catholic.*

Karen: *So … if I'm not a Christian?*

Gordon: *Christianity is very important to me.*

Karen: *I'm not Christian and looking for someone more lax about religion. I would recommend that you list that your faith is very important to you on the profile, so you avoid possible confusion from other ladies. Best of luck dating!*

Gordon: *You too. No hard feelings.*

This is a textbook example of why it's important to broach the subject of faith as soon as possible—particularly if it's not listed on a profile. If I had taken this conversation further without confirming what his religious beliefs were, I would have wasted both our time and energy pursuing something that had no possibility of success. It was merely an effective weeding of prospects.

The single most important thing that holds a relationship together for the long term—the *glue*—is a mutuality of values, beliefs, and world views between the two partners. Chemistry is essential and has to be there in some way in a romantic relationship, but as we all know, it can fade quickly after the honeymoon phase. What makes a relationship stick for the long term is for both partners to have common ground in their most important beliefs. When it comes to beliefs, opposites do *not* attract.

Question 4: What do I hate?

Hate may seem out of place in a book about love. But identifying what you hate offers two important benefits. First, if you *hate* something that a potential date or partner is, does, possesses, believes, or loves, you're headed for problems. Knowing early can save you a lot of lost time.

Second, as much as having mutual interests with your partner is essential, strong mutual dislikes can bring people a lot closer, too. Sometimes, the more intense the hatred, the better the relationship will be because the couple will develop a deeper bond, united by their dislike or hatred of the same things.

One of my former co-workers, Katy, hates—I mean *hates*—a certain U.S. president (Let's just call him "President T" for ease of reference). She is very liberal and has no issue with sharing her feelings in conversation or on social media.

Her feelings are so strong that she has a genuine belief that anyone who does *not* share her hatred for President T is a complete and utter idiot. A potential partner of Katy's who voted for him (much less might again), is boarding the dating Titanic; at some point, he's going down.

Some "hatreds" initially sound trivial, more like a "pet peeve," but end up being not so trivial after all. My relative, Wes, is *always* punctual—usually early—and expects the same from everyone in his life, including a partner. Wes, however, is married to Maria, for whom punctuality is generally not even on the radar. At first glance, this may seem trivial—after all, it's just "being a little late" from time to time, not a fundamental difference in beliefs, right? *Wrong.* Wes may have found it cute during the honeymoon phase when Maria came rushing breathlessly into a restaurant with all the reasons she was twenty minutes late. Perhaps it was forgivable when she thought their appointment with the lawyer to get their wills done was an hour *later* than the actual time of (at a rate of $300 per hour). But as most pet peeves tend to do, this one grew and became something more. When Maria walked in late to Wes' daughter's piano recital, distracting everyone, including his daughter, the peeve transformed into a deep source of marital problems.

Still, a shared hatred can also be genuinely bonding. One of my friends has been married for over twenty years, and he and his wife share many likes and dislikes. But the one thing they both particularly hate is animal breeders. They have a passion for rescue animals, but they loathe the idea of anyone profiting from dog and cat reproduction when there is such an overpopulation of animals in need of good homes. As a result, they've formed a non-profit organization devoted to finding homes for rescues, neutering animals, and educating the public about the dark side of dog and cat breeding. This shared passion and hatred has brought them even closer in their marriage.

Now it's your turn. List your top ten hates, dislikes, or pet peeves:

1)

2)

3)

4)

5)

6)

7)

8)

9)

10)

Feels better getting all that out, doesn't it?

Question 5: What are my favorite interests, activities, and hobbies?

This should be an easy one: list ten interests, activities, hobbies, or things you like to do in your spare time. Think exercising, attending sporting events, painting, traveling, playing the guitar, cooking, going to live concerts, working on cars, going to casinos, or anything that gets your juices flowing! Be specific; instead of just saying "music," take the extra step and write what particular type of music you like. One of my friends was excited to meet a prospective date because the man had listed that he was a music lover and had been to over a hundred concerts. It turned out, however, that she was a rock fan and he loved country music, which she seriously disliked, maybe even hated! Being specific sooner would have saved them much time and emotional turmoil.

My top ten interests, activities, or hobbies are:

1)
2)
3)
4)
5)
6)
7)
8)
9)
10)

If you struggle to come up with ten, then start with five. Remember, almost everyone likes TV or movies, music, food, entertainment, sports, and travel; just writing these won't be enough. Instead, narrow further to specific genres, cuisines, destinations, or categories. If you struggle to come up with ten interests, consider exploring new activities with your friends, or alone—like hiking, cooking, joining a book club, or attending a wine tasting. Pay attention to what you *really* enjoy. (And you never know who you'll meet!)

As with so much of the *Matched* approach, brutal honesty will serve you in the long term. For example, I don't like sports—not on TV, not live, not at all. I once attended a baseball game at Yankee Stadium that everyone raved about; I was bored out of my mind. The only thing I enjoyed about that day was the boat ride to and from the stadium, looking across the deck at the New York City skyline, and feeling the breeze off the East River.

Knowing that, why in the world would I list on my profile that I like watching sports? You might think it would attract more guys because guys like sports, but even if that *were* true, do I really want to start a relationship with a lie? Do I want to set both my partner and me up for extreme disappointment when I get angry at him for giving me 50-yard-line tickets for my birthday? Do I want to be tortured during the honeymoon phase by attending games with him, bored silly, before the truth finally comes out? My point is this: your goal isn't to simply attract *more* dates. It's about attracting *better* ones, who are a fit for you. It's quality over quantity.

You can not—and should not—fake passion, preferences, likes, and dislikes. If you are passionate about your partner, you can work to develop an interest in the activities he or she enjoys. Over time, you may even develop your passion for those things, too, and come to enjoy them together even if you would have never done so on your own.

I am deeply passionate about salsa dancing. I love it. Ideally, I would like my partner to join me in this activity, too; making an effort to learn and dance with me would enhance our relationship significantly. But it's not a deal-breaker. It's a gift to a relationship when one partner chooses to be open-minded about an activity that the other is passionate about, but it doesn't have to be a requirement. I can find other salsa partners, and there's value in doing things separately and having individual interests. The bullshit Hallmark Channel fantasy of liking and doing all the same things is simply not sustainable. If my partner has two left feet, or simply does not want to go dancing but would rather go out with his friends, that's fine. The rule is one of up-front honesty so that you can find a balance that works for both of you.

* * *

If you answered all five questions and did so *honestly*, you should have a much better idea of who you really are. If you did not complete all the questions, do not move to the next chapter until you do!

Don't worry about finding the perfect answer. Let go of the excuses. "I don't have time," is *bullshit*. Putting a little upfront time into understanding yourself and your needs might be the best time you ever spend. A few extra minutes now will make it much easier for you to select and attract a quality and *lasting* match.

Now, enough about *you* and on to *them*. It's time to start defining your ideal match!

CHAPTER 4

Your Ideal Partner

Too often we forget that an ideal partner is someone who enhances an already full existence.

–Mariella Frostrup

Take a moment now and pat yourself on the back for completing your internal lists! You are yet one step closer to attaining your dream relationship.

Before you jump into the deep end of the dating pool, it's time to consider your wishes—and *non*-wishes—regarding your ideal partner. You'll be wiser and waste far less time on the wrong suitors if you can first articulate *specifically* what type of person is truly your match. Better still, you'll avoid the "chemistry risk" discussed in the introduction that's so common in new relationships. When your dates match your desires, you can allow yourself to enjoy the chemistry that comes with meeting new *compatible* people instead of worrying that it might mislead you.

This chapter will help you explore what it is you truly want in a partner, farther beyond just "chemistry." Open your mind, settle in, and get ready to write!

Partner "Wish List"

Your first question is simple: *What kind of partner do I want to attract?*

This is where many people stumble; it may be simple, but it's not necessarily easy. Yes, almost everyone is going to say *loyal, smart,* and *good-looking,* and some of those may indeed be in your top ten. But before you decide, take some time. Think first about who *you* really are deep down inside. Revisit your lists from the previous chapters if you don't remember all the special qualities that only you have. (You are awesome, are you not?)

Close your eyes and return to your memories of the best relationships throughout your life—not just romantic ones, but friends, and family, too. What kind of people make you feel your best or bring out the best in you? What qualities do they have that you like most about them? Think about how those qualities complement and match with yours.

At first blush, you may think you want someone with the same characteristics as you. That certainly can be important. Everyone needs things in common with those they care about, and some of those are absolute musts. Integrity is one of my top values, so I would list that as one of the top values in my partner wish list. But on the other hand, since I can be high-maintenance, I mesh best with laid back guys; *easygoing* (rather than someone similarly high-maintenance) would be one of my most desirable characteristics in a partner as well.

Take a moment to think about at least ten qualities and characteristics that you want your partner to have. Remember: this is a wish list! Let go of your ideas about what you might "deserve" or what kind of partner you feel you can attract. This is about what's *ideal.* It's time to let your mind run free.

My wish list for my ideal partner is:

1)
2)
3)
4)
5)
6)
7)
8)
9)
10)

How did you do? If you let yourself *truly* wish, then you likely had a hard time limiting your list to just ten things! If you struggled to come up with ten, it's time to let go and allow yourself to dream. Don't forget to think broadly. Your wish list can cover a wide array of categories, like beliefs, personality traits, values, physical characteristics, hatreds, and interests.

As with all of these lists, you *must* be honest with yourself. If you want your partner to be a college graduate, write it down! If you want your partner to be a particular ethnicity, list that. Women, if you really, really want a partner who makes substantially more money than you, then don't be ashamed to admit it and put it on your list! Men, if you want a woman who is slim and physically fit, then *own it*. Don't feel guilty. This is your private list; add anything *you* want. Knowing *what* you want will help you get closer to getting it.

Let's take another run at the list and let at least a handful more wishes out onto the page.

My wish list for my ideal partner is:

11)
12)
13)
14)
15)
16)
17)
18)
19)
20)

Your Partner "Must" List

Once you've created your top twenty partner qualities and characteristics wish list, it's time to narrow that list to your absolute *musts*. What is essential? What's non-negotiable in terms of beliefs, personality traits, values, physical characteristics, hatreds, and interests?

My partner, for example, *must* be intelligent, generous, and open-minded about religion. Yes, I *prefer* a partner with blue eyes who likes to dance, but those are just wishes, not *musts*. Wishes are preferences. Musts are something that you can't live without. Take a moment now to list your top five *musts*.

My top five partner musts *are:*

1)
2)
3)
4)
5)

This list of your top five will give you a clear focus on the things that are *the* most important and non-negotiable while going through the next steps of building your profile and screening potential matches.

Your Partner "Do-Not-Wish" List

A funny quirk of human nature is that it's often easier for us to identify what we don't like than it is to articulate what we *do*, which explains all the hard work in the previous three chapters!

That should make the job of creating your do-not-wish list easier, but it doesn't mean you should give this section short-shrift. Before you jump into list-making, let's look at the subtleties—there's more to consider here than you might realize.

Usually, when you encounter characteristics you dislike in someone, you tend to know immediately that that person is not a good match for you. You're able to weed them out effortlessly and move on. I am not a fan of "Debbie Downers" (or "Donnie Downers," if you will)—those who incessantly complain or wallow in negativity. I can barely tolerate it in friends or family, much less a partner. I would likewise never date someone who smokes, not even occasionally, so that's on my list too. Couch potatoes are also out for me as well, simply because I am very active and value my health. I don't want my mountain-climbing trip in Patagonia hindered by my partner's need for an oxygen tank!

You can likely come up with a similar list of peeves and dislikes. But before you jump to screen out prospective partners, consider that these things may also be works-in-progress, especially if you haven't dated in a while.

Dale is a self-proclaimed neat freak and obsessive about cleaning and organization. He thought he could *never* be with a messy, disorganized woman. When Dale met Lauren, they hit it off right away. They had several dates, but red flags soon began to fly. One night, as Dale helped Lauren look for her car keys, he was startled by the "condition" of her purse. "It was no wonder she couldn't find her keys," he told me later, "with all the *crap* floating around in the bottom of her bag: open tubes of lipstick, tissues, change, a small bottle of Gorilla Glue, a couple of broken off acrylic nails, innumerable receipts, etc."

When Dale finally visited her home, things were no better. There was no question that Lauren was no neat freak. She was the opposite.

But Dale had learned something along the way. For all her messiness, Lauren possessed many qualities that were extremely important to him. She shared his political views, she had a strong sex drive, she did not mind that he had young children, and she had a great sense of humor. Dale's mental do-not-wish list had led him to assume he couldn't tolerate someone who lacked cleanliness and organization, but he was wrong. For the right person, he was willing to compromise.

The Hidden Side of Your Wish Lists

In Dr. Harville Hendrix's brilliant book, *Getting the Love You Want*, he describes that during his career as a therapist, he found that many people were subconsciously attracted to negative characteristics they experienced in their childhood, specifically those of their parents, siblings, or caregivers. Time after time, people would make the same mistakes, moving from one partner to another, only to find the same challenges. The very things they should have had on their do-not-wish lists, in other words, were the very things they were subconsciously attracted to.

This was a revelation to me. One of the characteristics I most disliked in my ex was that he was self-absorbed and could not usually see things from my point of view. Now, it brought back countless childhood memories of my mother, who shared similar behavior and characteristics. I would never have put *self-absorbed, judgmental,* or *close-minded* on my partner wish list, yet here I was going into my marriage wholly unaware that I had been subconsciously doing just that. I'd been attracted to someone with the same negative characteristics as my mother. He also had my father's temper issues!

Instead of seeking out those traits, I should probably have listed them high on my do-not-wish list; the problem was that I had no idea I was even attracted to them.

Take the time to think about the most undesirable and negative characteristics of your parents, early childhood caregivers, and former partners. As they say, history tends to repeat itself. How many sexually or physically abused girls grow up to be battered wives? How many battered wives move from one abusive relationship to another just like it, or worse? Think of men who are not physically abused, but are beaten down by an overbearing and controlling woman; if that relationship ends, they inexplicably seem to move on to another domineering or abusive partner.

It's a counterintuitive idea. Could we really be unknowingly attracted to and seeking out the very things we think we want to avoid? The answer is yes, and the first step toward a solution is to explicitly state the *must-nots* of your future relationships. This way, it will be easier to weed out potential partners early on in the process without getting hurt by the same "type" because you get to choose *consciously*.

Here are some common examples of things which are often

undesirable in a potential partner: jealousy, bad temper, hygiene issues, excessive alcohol or drug use, vulgarity, low self-esteem, infidelity, lack of humor, excessive debt, obesity, stupidity, baldness (hey, this is your private list, and the key is to be honest), lack of faith, immaturity, politically opposite beliefs, low sex drive, bad teeth, arrogance, laziness, racism, bad grammar, mental or physical health issues, and anything else that is in your list of *must-nots*.

Some of these may seem trivial to you. Others will qualify for your list. The point is that there is a long list of things that can be polarizing between two people. Your job is to identify them as early as possible before you invest time and emotional energy in a relationship. Again, you must create your list *honestly*, regardless of whether you think some choices are superficial or not.

Ladies, if you know that you could never be satisfied with a man who is shorter than you, *write it down*! Gentlemen, if a whiny, nagging woman makes you lose your mind, no matter how good-looking she is—well, you know the drill. Must nots or dislikes are not likely to be fixable or go away.

Exercise: Create Your Must-Not-Have List

My wish list for the attributes my partner must not have includes:

1)
2)
3)
4)
5)
6)
7)

8)

9)

10)

Just as with your partner wish list, you may find you want to keep on writing past the first ten. First, however, let's revisit the things that at first you may think are just pet peeves or bad habits, but in your mind, don't qualify as deal-breakers. They're probably the items from the do-not-wish list you created earlier.

Believe me, a simple little "habit" can easily qualify as a deal-breaker—in particular, those habits that tend to escalate over time. As I shared earlier, smoking is an absolute no for me. I came across the profile of a man who looked interesting and loved to snow ski (double bonus points since I love skiing as well). However, although he said "never" to the smoking question in his profile, there was a photo of him where he had a cigar in his mouth. Rather than wait and see, I directly asked him about it while messaging.

Karen: *Hi Kirk, I also love to ski and go 2-3 times a year, mostly to Colorado. I noticed you are chewing on a cigar in one of your photos but you list on your profile that you do not smoke. Which is it?*

Kirk: *I don't smoke.*

Karen: *So how come you are chewing on a cigar?*

Kirk: *I smoke cigars when I'm at a cigar bar with friends every now and then.*

Karen: *You just said you don't smoke?!?*

Kirk: *I don't consider cigars "smoking." It's only occasionally, and I hate cigarette smoke.*

Karen: *I hate cigarettes and cigars and any type of smoking. Sorry, but yuck!*

I unmatched without even waiting on a response. For me,

the decision was easy. Smoking is on my "must-not" list. It's a deal-breaker, in any amount.

For some, however, casual smoking might be fine. As might casual alcohol or drug use. But what if that casual use escalates? Will it still be fine then?

Many people have issues with alcohol and substance abuse—because they have a history with someone with alcohol issues, or because they are a recovering alcoholic. Casual use may not seem like a deal-breaker, but it's wise to ask yourself if that's true in the long run. Will it affect your happiness if it escalates? If it stays the same? Can you picture decades with a person with those habits?

Substance use and abuse is not something everyone wants to advertise when dating, but whether it's a habit you have or a habit you can't tolerate, it's best for everyone to be forthright. If you absolutely do not want such a partner, be clear. If you do far more than socially drink or you smoke weed daily, be honest and don't try to match with someone who clearly cannot tolerate that. If you're unwilling to disclose your private information, at least be considerate and don't even start a conversation with someone who has clearly stated that those things are deal-breakers.

Likewise, political orientation can be highly contentious in relationships—if not immediately, then over time. Many people are so entrenched in their political beliefs that they stick to friends and significant others who share similar viewpoints.

It is, of course, possible to have a good relationship when one partner is a far-left Democrat and the other is a right-wing Republican. But to develop a healthy relationship under these conditions, both partners must have deep respect for the other and their beliefs—just as with religion. Some couples will decide to leave politics alone altogether, where some will try to have open dialogue even if they disagree. Whatever a couple decides is okay, as long as both parties are comfortable with this arrangement and can respect the other and accept that the other's viewpoint is just as valid.

What does this mean for dating? As with all your work so far, the goal is to look inward and decide in advance how important the issue is.

In my case, for example, I could never date a person who does not believe in equal rights for the LGBTQ community (or any person with a different sexual orientation). When it comes to politics, I always try to learn more about points of view other than mine, and I am open to political discussion, as well as open to dating people with different political beliefs. Personally, however, I could not respect someone who likes President T. It would be one thing if my partner agreed with his politics and economic policy. But if he liked Trump as a person (who I view as a narcissistic, racist, womanizer who lacks empathy and common sense, among other things), that person would be a complete mismatch for me. That is not simply a "checked box," i.e., "You like President T., therefore I do not like you." It's that it almost certainly represents a conflict in fundamental values which, for me, include empathy and compassion—the exact thing we tried to avoid by using the questions of Chapter 3.

Revisit your do-not-wish list now, and consider any other traits or habits that don't seem like deal-breakers. Is there anything else you'd like to add to your must-not list?

11)

12)

13)

14)

15)

16)

17)

18)

19)

20)

So far, we've mentioned nothing about family relationships and situations as a no-go—has it come up in your list?

If you haven't considered it already, the time has come. It's such an important topic, in fact, that it gets its very own chapter next!

CHAPTER 5

Family Dynamics

In family life, love is the oil that eases friction, the cement that binds closer together, and the music that brings harmony.

–Friedrich Nietzsche

In the last four chapters, you've taken the first steps toward finding your dream relationship. You found your personal *why*, assessed your relationship readiness, took a close look at your own nature, and described your ideal partner.

There's a good chance that somewhere in those early preparatory stages—or *everywhere*, for that matter—the topic of family came up, particularly children. Before you enter into any serious dating considerations, it's time to give the subject more careful thought.

I know, I know. We haven't even set up your profile yet or gone on a first date. Do you *really* have to worry about something as deep and complex as family now? The answer is an absolute yes. After questions of faith and values, family is the single most important topic of discussion (and contention) for potential partners.

The term, however, covers a lot of ground. The most obvious territory is children. Do you have kids? If not, do you want them? Are you open to a relationship with someone who has children, even if you do not want any of your own? Would you consider being with someone who does not want to have children?

But children are just one part of the family dynamics picture. What about former family? Would you be okay with dating someone who is still married but separated? Would you have a problem being with someone who has been married a number of times? What if a potential partner has a parent or other adult family member living with them? Or grandchildren they are raising?

And what about exes and children? Would it be a problem for you if the other parent (the ex of your potential partner) is heavily involved in the children's lives? What if the other parent is not involved at all, and you potentially would become "Mom" or "Dad?"

Be sure you don't shy away from scenarios that make you feel guilty or uncomfortable, either. What if a potential partner had a severely handicapped child who required 24/7 attention? Or a biracial child, or an adopted child of another race? Or a child at home with serious discipline or behavioral issues?

You may find many of these questions easy to answer. Others may be more challenging. The point is not how difficult they are, but whether you ask them in the first place—both of yourself and of potential partners. In the sections that follow, that's exactly what you'll be learning how to do.

New Children? Old Children? No Children?

In the early years of dating, the various challenges of kids in relationships can seem distant or unimportant, but over time they can develop into prime deal-breakers that destroy long-term relationships or prevent them from ever forming at all.

If you're reading this book, you are probably at least open to a long-term relationship, if not craving it. (By now, you've likely realized that if you're looking for a friend with benefits, you don't need me!) But if a lasting relationship is what you want, then a discussion about children is absolutely what you *need*. Now is a time to revisit your *why* and honestly assess the potential long-term with someone in the context of family—both yours and theirs.

First, it's extremely important to disclose whether you already have children (and their ages, and whether they live with you or not). If you don't have kids, be clear about whether you want to one day. Holding back such life-altering information is not only irrational but horribly unfair. People don't always set out to mislead, but a fear of being rejected will sometimes keep people from revealing this side of their life. But starting any potential relationship with a lie, even by omission, is a bad idea, particularly for something this important.

Consider, for example, a potential partner who absolutely does not want children, but you have three. He will never consider dating you seriously—there's no long-term potential there, and you both are just wasting time if you do not make immediate and full disclosures.

Do *not* try to fool yourself that if you look good and are smart and funny, he'll be so attracted to you that he will forget all about your three munchkins. Your full house, and his permanent studio, metaphorically speaking, are never going to fit.

As those with children know, life with kids requires a very different lifestyle and level of commitment, particularly in the early years. Parents often plan days in advance even just to go out to dinner and a movie; the childless can spontaneously jump on a plane for a weekend in Vegas. There's no right or wrong, but there's a night and day difference in routine and requirements.

There are so many possible scenarios here. Someone with several children of their own who does not want any more (of their own or others). Someone with no children who desperately wants them, but only children of their own. Someone who has children of their own and truly really does not care either way if a potential partner does or does not have children. Someone whose children are grown and at a minimum wants their partner's children out of the nest as well. Someone with no children who never wants their own or anyone else's. Someone with multiple children who wants multiple more. The list goes on.

The approach, however, is the same in all cases. You need to ask yourself the hard questions—not just before you say "I do," not just before your first date, not even just before you begin messaging, but before you even post your profile! And when you start dating, you need to ask those questions of potential partners, too.

In addition to your personal preferences, you also need to give serious thought to the basic logistics of everyday life. If you have four children at home and he has three, what size (and cost) of home is needed to accommodate everyone? What if you have opposite-sex children of approximately the same age—will that be awkward for them? What if you have same-sex children close to the same age? Will that be challenging? Is there potential for conflict and power struggles not just between kids, but between you and your partner?

What if one or more of your partner's children absolutely despise you? (Or, if you are honest, that you despise them?)

Even if you get along marvelously with your partner, children bring *endless* other complications with them: wanting attention from their own parent, fighting with their new step-siblings, fighting with *you*. And even if you are fortunate enough to avoid these types of major issues, remember that *you* may be the one who has to drive them to soccer practice on Saturday mornings when you just want to sleep in!

Consider, too, the ages of children. Are they still in diapers, needing lots of attention, or are they two years from going to college? Someone who has one child a year from going to college may not want a partner with kids aged five and two—or they may; the point is you need to *know* what you want from a partner, and you need to disclose this on your profile so that it is easier for someone to weed you out if they are not interested in your specific family situation. Remember: we want quality over quantity, fact over fiction.

This can take some exploration, both inner and outer. Initially, I thought I'd be fine with a partner with small children, but after dating a man who fell into that category, I realized that this required a gargantuan effort on my part. This man had four children, all under the age of twelve. Not only did that reduce the time and energy he had for me, but it also reduced the time and energy I had for my own daughter. Being a great mother to my daughter is my top priority, and I knew I needed to conserve much time and energy for her as I could. It simply wasn't going to work. Later, I modified that item on my profile, and I now refuse to date someone with more than two young children.

This goes both ways, too. I met Michael through a dating app, and although I was forty-four at the time and he was fifty-nine, I found him to be very attractive, not just physically, but in the way his profile was written. We messaged a few times and then had a long phone call, during which I learned that he had been married twice and had no children of his own. I immediately asked him if he would be open to having an eight-year-old (my daughter) in a relationship; he said "sure," and in fact, he had lived with a woman for two years who had a young son. He said he knew what he was getting into in case we hit it off.

That sounded promising, and I agreed to meet him for drinks, which we then followed with dinner, where I learned that Michael had two successful businesses. He was smart, accomplished, and honest, with high energy and presence. He was also highly intelligent, a world traveler, a car enthusiast, a foodie, and had a long list of other great qualities I really liked. Better yet, Michael appeared to genuinely like me, and the feeling was mutual. I felt genuine chemistry between us—something that seemed extremely rare as I had felt those magical "butterflies" on so few dates.

We had a couple of more dates, but before the next one, I had some issues arranging a babysitter. Even though Michael rescheduled an earlier date twice due to business and travel commitments, the moment I had to change because of childcare issues, he lamented: *Karen, I thought about this for a while. Although I like you a lot and I am really attracted to you, both physically and to the person you are, at this point in my life, I want someone without young children who will be able to spend weekends with me and travel with me. I want you to know this now before anyone gets really hurt.*

You know what? I actually thanked him. I respected Michael for telling me as soon as he realized that it wasn't the right fit for him. I was elated to know that he did like me and respect me, but that the limitations were purely practical.

Since Michael, I ask men upfront if they are okay not only with me having a daughter, but with me having primary custody. While it has been a deterrent for some, it is so much better to know this in advance before wasting time and effort by going on a date, feeling attraction, and then feeling disappointed, or worse, later.

Kids matter in relationships. If you like someone, but you can't learn the truth from their profile, address it on your first in-person date. No exceptions.

Parenting Styles

Once you are past any deal-breakers around children, you like each other, and things move on to second and third dates and beyond, you can begin to discuss your parenting styles, relevant values, and how you might raise your kids in a blended family. This is definitely *not* first date material—after all, you're still trying to figure out if you like each other enough to have a second. However, it is a perfectly logical and suitable choice for subsequent dates.

Eventually, you'll need to know these parenting-type details about a potential partner. It's critical for a lasting relationship. And it goes both ways: be ready to ask questions, but also to answer back, and do it honestly. Are you lax or strict with discipline? What about nutrition? After-school activities? Policies about the use of electronic devices? Private or public schools? Curfew? There is a near-endless list of topics to cover, so you may as well get started.

I know couples who absolutely will not allow their children to have electronics during school days, and others who shove a tablet into their kids' hands to keep them quiet on any day of the week. If you aren't on the same page about these things, the sooner you find out, the better. Not every difference is a deal-breaker, but the more you discuss things, the better off you'll be.

Brace yourself, though, because blended families can be quite difficult to manage. Consider how it will feel to have, "You're not my Mom (or Dad)!" flung at you; more important still, think about what your expectations of your partner will be when this occurs.

Most people in the dating arena have baggage. For some it is emotional and hidden, and for others, it is in the form of a three-year-old kicking and screaming on the floor in Target. How would you behave if this happened to you and how do you expect your potential partner to behave? When kids are involved, put on your seatbelt and get ready for the ride!

I also recommend disclosing or listing your custody arrangements, at least in general terms. In my case, I have primary custody, and my ex has our daughter on Thursdays and every other weekend. Many people have a 50/50 arrangement. This isn't just about the long-term—it can be quite important even for dating. During the workweek, almost everyone is busy; generally, the weekends are the best time to unwind and spend quality time with your partner. If one, much less both of you, has primary custody of your child(ren), it can take tremendous effort just to plan a date, much less a weekend away. You'll be hard-pressed to find quality time with someone who has their kids on opposite weekends from you.

Definition of "Single"

Without even venturing into open or polyamorous relationships (next section!), it's important to determine what someone really means by *single*. Think of the possibilities and potential dynamics associated with *never married* versus *widowed*, or *divorced* versus *separated*. In each case, "single" may be accurate, but each one also raises more questions:

- Why, at fifty-seven years old, have you never married?
- Were all seven of your divorces *really* your husbands' faults? Or could the problem be *you*?
- If you're married but separated, why can you only see me for lunch? And why won't you give me your phone number?
- You're 40 and never had a committed, long-term relationship? *What is wrong with you?*
- Your wife's funeral was *when*?

Lest you think I'm joking, consider a friend of a friend, Robert, who had been married to his high school sweetheart, Dina, for some twenty years. They had two children and appeared to have an idyllic life until Dina unexpectedly died in her forties of a severe asthma attack. From all appearances, Robert was a good person, and his fidelity to Dina had never been in question. Yet after her funeral, Robert immediately began making romantic advances towards numerous women, even to nurses he had met while they cared for Dina before she was taken off life support. Not only did Robert begin dating someone else very quickly, but he also remarried within a few short months of Dina's death.

The new relationship was, for the most part, a disaster. Robert's children still deeply mourned the loss of their mother, and not only despised their new stepmom Patricia, but also resented their father for jumping into a new relationship so quickly.

Robert, for his part, was in his fifties and did not want any more children. He had told this to the childless and previously unmarried Patricia (who was a good bit younger than him). She claimed not to be able to have children, so that was fine; as it turned out, she could, and she did. Robert, now in his mid-fifties, became the father of an infant and harbored a sneaking suspicion that Patricia manipulated him into having a child.

When Robert and Patricia married, Patricia had a career, and Robert owned his own successful business that generated a good income. Now that Patricia had a baby, and Robert could support their household on his salary, she quit her job and began a less-than-enthusiastic network marketing "career." The sex that was hot and heavy when they were dating became nonexistent after their child was born. When Patricia suffered from post-partum depression and became increasingly meaner to Robert and the children from his first marriage who still lived at home with them, things spiraled downward even further.

Ultimately, Patricia had an affair, and when Robert found out, she was the one to immediately file for divorce. They had a protracted and expensive custody fight, during which she accused him of everything under the sun (including even that he had molested his own child). Although Robert ultimately did get primary custody, the emotional and financial toll was tremendous. His legal fees approached $100,000, and he had to pay alimony. And, because of a shared child, two people who can no longer stand each other are connected forever.

For Robert and everyone involved, the new relationship was *too soon*. When a potential partner is separated, divorced, or widowed, it's important for you to know how recently the relationship ended. You'll also want to know *why*.

In this regard, death is clear; you can focus on how long ago it was, how well the person is dealing with it, and their *why* for dating. In the instance of divorce, however, you'll eventually want to try and filter out the deeper *why*. Don't expect most people to simply accept all blame, pand rarely is it *all* just one spouse's fault.

But if your potential suitor Casanova has been married four times, and admits to having cheated on all four wives, you might want to dig deeper. No matter the excuse (*She wouldn't have sex with me. I wasn't in love with her anymore. I just can't keep the women off of me!*), you might well expect history to repeat itself.

Think long and hard before becoming seriously involved with someone whose relationship ended recently, whatever the reason. While some rebound relationships make it, those who are just out of serious long-term relationships generally need time to heal and move on. The timeframe varies from person to person, and it can often take as much as a year or two to resolve and heal.

My divorce itself took over two years. And while I was completely over the marriage two years prior to its formal end, the entire process, which was highly contested, took a huge emotional toll. I wasn't really ready to date until I first learned how to live alone and reconnect with myself. I needed to understand, and to love, the woman I was and had become.

Time matters. It might not take two years to heal from a three-month relationship, but the reverse isn't true—dating within three months after a two-year marriage might be a recipe for disaster.

There are no rules here. But it's common to need six months to two years, depending on the length of the relationship and how or why it ended. Only a minority of divorces are amicable. Many can be quite bitter and leave plenty of emotional baggage. A relationship ending in death requires its own time to process, too. No matter how a relationship ends, expect that it will take time for both you and potential partners to process the idea of being single and all that it entails.

Open Relationships

If you noticed "Open Relationships" in the Table of Contents of this book and rolled your eyes, you're in for a surprise. They are much more common today than many realize. Some apps, like *Bumble, Tinder,* and *OkCupid,* do not restrict users to monogamous relationships—you can list "non-monogamous" or even "polyamorous" on your profile. Other apps, such as *Match,* prohibit listing a profile if someone is in a relationship, regardless of marital status.

I once had a situation on *Match* where I was messaging with a guy who I had lost interest in, but he was very nice, and I did not want to hurt his feelings. So, my (admittedly untruthful) way of dealing with it was to tell him that I had just found a boyfriend, but I wished him well. Shortly after, *Match* terminated my account, stating I had violated their terms of use. I had to contact them to reinstate it, and I learned a good lesson about simply being honest.

So, with "honesty is the best policy" as a guide, please disclose your open relationship interests front and center. This is particularly important for a couple of reasons. One, it makes it easy for people like me, who are only interested in a monogamous relationship, to quickly move on to someone who is as well. And two, honesty means that people who *are* looking for an open relationship don't have to read between the lines to find it.

For many people, an ambiguous or non-normative relationship status is at least a red flag, if not a red line. They may not want to date you if you are married, or even if separated and in the process of divorce. For us monogamous folks, this red line is even more pronounced if you are in a committed relationship—even if your partner or spouse is fully aware of you also dating other people (referred to as "ethically non-monogamous"). You absolutely should not blame someone for this, any more than you should fault or judge someone for being polyamorous, or gay, or Catholic. Dating is *all* about individual desires and prerogatives—you get to decide what you want, and so does everyone else. Being upfront about your intentions and status is not just a practical approach to finding your dream relationship, but it's the right thing to do.

Pets

This topic could almost have been included in the discussion of children because, for many people, pets *are* their children!

It's a topic that should give you *paws* (pause) for thought. Some people will not even date you if you have a cat, much less if your friends lovingly refer to you as The Cat Lady. Others will question whether you truly have a heart if you can't produce your PETA membership card on demand.

Of course, there are many people who are somewhere in between. For the right person, they might even accept the hairballs, leg-humping, and shoe-chewing of your beloved pet. Regardless, if the goal is a long-term, quality partnership, then potential furry family members must be considered as part of family dynamics.

My sister is a perfect example. She is extremely allergic to cat hair, and even getting close to cats causes her to stream tears and sneeze profusely. From a purely practical standpoint, she can't date a man who has cats for any long-term period. Similarly, if you have two Siamese cats and your potential partner has three German Shepherds and a Parakeet, this may not be a great mix. (Unless you live on a farm, then you just need a goat and a pig to complete your ensemble. Go for it!)

Mark, who I now lovingly refer to as The Dog Guy, was a sweet, witty, and intelligent man who adored me. He constantly told me how gorgeous, unique, and smart I was. (I love a man who tells the truth!) He had been through a difficult divorce, but had two kids and seemed to be a great dad. When we started dating, he was checking all the boxes!

After several dates, Mark invited me to his place for the evening. When I walked in, I was shocked to see how filthy it was. His originally light-beige carpets had been stained a very dark gray, and there was pug hair *everywhere*.

Now, I can live with a little mess, like dishes sitting in the sink overnight, because I'm too tired to load the dishwasher after a dinner party. But I want my surroundings, both at home and work, to be clean and organized. Living in a dirty environment bothers me to my core. When I walked into Mark's place, I was disgusted.

Before I had a chance to order a hazmat suit or see anything else in the disaster zone, or Mark's living room, he led me to his bedroom. His pug, Henry, followed right behind. I assumed Mark would shoo the dog out, but instead, he closed the door of the bedroom with Henry inside. I asked, only half-jokingly, "Does Henry sleep in here too?" while looking around for his dog bed. Mark replied, "Yeah, he sleeps with me in the bed."

Apparently, for over a year before Mark's divorce, he had been exiled to the couch. During that time, Henry became his "bed buddy." I know the comfort that a pet can bring to their owner's life, and I have no doubt that this was particularly true during that trying and lonely time for Mark. But when I looked at Mark's bed sheets, originally black and now mostly white and gray with Henry's hair, my sexy feelings went out the window, and Mark went into the figurative doghouse.

I asked Mark if he'd be willing to give up sleeping with Henry when we are together.

His response? "I need to think about it."

I did not.

Some of you may be thinking, *Come on, Karen; quit being so obsessive. It's a dog, and Mark loved him!* That may be true. But I'm *me*, and I know that sharing a bed with a fur-shedding, drooling, snoring pug isn't going to work. Just as it was Mark's prerogative to choose Henry as his bed-buddy rather than me, I got to choose, too.

The point of this story is not to criticize but demonstrate how deeply some people love their pets. And like everything else, the things we value most need to be clarified upfront.

Exercise: Clarifying Family Dynamics

This chapter is intended to spur you to again dig deep into your beliefs and values in the context of family.

Here are some questions to prompt you:

- Do you have no children and desperately want to?
- Do you want a relationship where you and your partner live together in a blended household with all the kids?
- Do you want to maintain separate residences, see each other on the weekends, and occasionally take family vacations together?
- Do you want to have more children, or are you done?
- Is someone who has been married more than a certain number of times a deal-breaker for you, regardless of the reasons?
- If your ideal relationship is to live together in a blended household with your partner and be with him or her daily, but your partner's dream is to have their own place and only be with you from time-to-time, what relationship are you building, and with whom?

- How important is it to you for you and a partner to share similar beliefs about child-rearing (faith, discipline, education, etc.)?
- What if a partner wanted to live together but not get married?

Using these questions to guide you, take a few moments to think about your ideal relationship.

My ideal relationship, as far as living arrangements with my partner, is:

_____

_____

_____

_____

Regarding children, my ideal situation is:

_____

_____

_____

_____

Go all out. Write down every single one of your prerequisites. If the space provided here is not enough, keep writing elsewhere. Use your phone, more paper, or a computer file. But don't stop writing until you're done.

This is your relationship, your partner, and your life. You get to choose! Do not compromise. Once you are done, and only once you are done, move on to the next step.

CHAPTER 6

Your Basic Profile

Dear Past, thank you for all the lessons.
Dear Future, I'm ready.

-Unknown

Congratulations are definitely in order: you've reached a milestone! You have now finished the challenging but oh-so-necessary "inner job" of preparation. If you've done your homework, you should know:

- who you are and what you can offer to a partner
- what type of partner you want
- what kind of relationship you want
- your deal-breakers, and what you will and will not tolerate in a relationship

Pat yourself on the back! Pop a bottle of champagne! You are officially leaps and bounds ahead of most people who date, both online and offline.

Now, it's time to embark on the next phase of finding your dream relationship: to make the shift from your inner world to the outside one. (Yes, it gets much easier from here!)

You'll now begin to build a profile—one that attracts more matches while staying true to yourself. You'll compile your basic information, including age, height, kids, and interests, and also choose profile photos that attract as many potential leads as possible during the initial browsing phase.

But first, some words of caution. The term *catfisher* describes someone who creates fake profiles on social media and dating sites to trick people into believing they are someone else. There are a wide variety of reasons for this. Some people want to explore their sexual fantasies via messages, exchanged photos, and the like. Some catfishers simply want to toy with others. Worse, some are thieves, trying to entice you into sending them money or personal information.

Catfishing shouldn't keep you from dating—we'll look at how to screen prospective dates carefully in a later chapter—but for now, it's wise to simply be aware that the dating world has more than a few trouble spots.

When you take the first step to sign up with a dating app, it's wise to use a new email address that is solely for this purpose. Some apps, such as Match, send email notifications for each message or "like." Using a separate email address to sign up for dating apps, as well as to communicate with potential dates, has several benefits. First, you can hide your real identity from someone who you may later discover was a catfisher or undesirable for some other reason. (Don't use your real name in your email; use a pseudonym like *AtlantaBlonde2020@gmail.com*.) Second, it'll be easier to keep track of who you respond to and your communications with them. Finally, a separate email means the app won't bombard your personal or work email with messages. That can be particularly important if you take a break from dating or from using a particular service.

Some apps, like Bumble, don't use your email address, so you get all messages on the app itself. In those cases, it's much easier to turn off notifications for a period of time. While some people want to see every message or "like" the second it comes in, many people simply like to read their messages all at one time in the evening or over the weekend when they are less busy. I personally prefer to disable all push notifications to minimize distractions.

Photos Matter More than You Think

Your photos are *the* most important aspect of your profile, especially your main photograph. Approximately 50% of people are primarily visual, about 30% are auditory, and some 20% are kinesthetic (feeling and touching). Attraction is something that we experience on many levels, but the role of appearance is particularly strong in the early stages. That makes your photos worth the extra time and effort.

Most men are visual, and their brains light up like a Christmas tree when they see a woman they are attracted to. Men will like or "swipe right" if they find you attractive, even just *potentially* attractive. For those of you who are truly online dating virgins, I will be using "swipe right" to generically refer to selecting, showing interest, or "liking" someone on an online app, and "swipe left" to refer to passing over someone's profile, or *not* liking them. Women do the same, but tend to be more forgiving if a man is not entirely their physical type but meets other requirements such as a successful career, aligned views, or education level. Regardless of gender, your photo selection matters because you are trying to gain attention—and ultimately match with your ideal partner—with the images you choose. Remember the adage: *A picture is worth a thousand words.*

Let me be clear that this isn't a statement about beauty or relative attractiveness. The fact that photos matter—and they most certainly do—doesn't mean that you need to consider yourself beautiful on some external scale that involves comparing yourself to others. What it *does* mean is that you should make an effort to do your best with your photos.

This becomes abundantly clear when we look at the statistical tendencies of men versus women using dating apps. Most men swipe right (or left) based on photos only. Only later will they read a woman's profile if she swipes right on them as well. Conversely, many women will not swipe at all based on looks alone (unless the man's looks fall under the "no way in hell" category), and will generally read the man's profile.

As a result of these gender differences, men get significantly less right swipes than women. Therefore, a guy has to right-swipe through many women to find a few women who right-swipe him as well. This means, ladies, that we have the upper hand at this stage, and you should be sure to take advantage of it! Once you swipe right on a man, he will *then* probably take the time to read your profile and decide whether to engage or not.

Since men tend to swipe first and figure it out later, however, don't assume a right-swipe means immediate interest. This is simply the most basic screening step without a whole lot of thought, if any. (Beyond, perhaps, *Meh. I'd probably do her ...* SWIPE)

Your photos, then, are *the* single most important factor to generate right-swipes from potential suitors. After both of you swipe right, then the text of your profile is what becomes important for the man to figure out if there is potential interest. You need to lead with your photos. Don't expect a man to go digging to find your personality *first*. In this age of too many options, women act the same way in screening male photos so good photos are very important for men also.

What Makes a Photo Great

Before you choose which photos you'll use, let's look at some specific pointers. To begin, choose unique, interesting, and (of course) attractive photos. Make sure you use recent photos in various settings to give potential dates a mix of experiences that you enjoy and that reveal aspects of your personality. Remember that your main photo is the most important; many people will quickly swipe left or right based on it alone, without reading your profile. Right or wrong, many people are disqualified based on that one lone photograph.

Your main photo is the entry point. If that photograph is attractive, a suitor may look at your other photos, and if those pique their interest, they may read your profile. But it all starts with the first shot. Make it count. For those of you who are online enthusiasts, how many times have you quickly swiped left on a guy taking a selfie in a bathroom? And one with 1970s tiles, a dirty towel on the rack, and used Q-tips on the counter? Or worse, guys taking selfies in a public restroom? *Ewwww!* Why anyone would think that stuff is attractive is beyond me. There are plenty of ways to be different and memorable with your pictures, and you really will get more right-swipes without a toilet in the background!

So, step out of the bathroom, and let's get ready. To make sure your photos do their job, they need to meet four criteria. They must be *recent, real, high quality,* and *secure.*

Recent

I wish it wasn't necessary to state this outright, but make sure your photos are *recent*. As a general rule, consider anything within the last six months—certainly no more than a year. Your pictures should show you with the same basic hair style and color as you wear now. If you cut off your long brunette hair to above your shoulders just last week and bleached it blonde, then recent now means *any day since then but not before*.

Make sure you look like the same person in all of your photos. You want a date to recognize you when you walk into a restaurant. One of the most common comments I received from my dates was, "Wow! You look *exactly* like your photos!"

Whether you realize it or not, photos that are even two or three years old may make you look quite different. Your goal should be to look similar enough to your photos that you could be picked out of a lineup. (Let's hope it doesn't come to that, but you know what I mean.)

Real

Keep your photos authentic. Men, in particular, tell me that women use photos shot from angles that make their bodies look much slimmer or otherwise different than they actually are. *Don't do it*. I am not skinny by any means, but I am not fat either. Whatever you currently are, that is you—the *you* that he or she will meet if you actually go on a date. If a guy is expecting a thirty-five-year-old with a CrossFit body, he will be sorely disappointed to meet a fifty-year-old who looks like she might have eaten the woman in the photo. It's irrelevant whether you are at your optimal weight right now. What *is* relevant is to have a photo that represents how you look *today*, so that your date's expectation meets reality. It will always lead to disappointment if you look worse in person than in your photos.

Both men and women need to have at least one recent full-body shot, although I recommend more than one. If all the photos on a profile are close-up face shots, that may indicate that they are trying to hide something, most likely their weight. Most men and women don't care if a potential partner is a little overweight, and even if you are quite overweight, many partners will still find you attractive; remember, *those* are the ones you are looking for! Find a full-body photo or two where you feel attractive—even if you're carrying a few extra pounds. And bear in mind that according to research, a full-body photo in your profile will get you two to three times as many likes as just a face shot—*regardless of your weight.*

While it may be women who are more prone to be misleading with our profile pictures, men can be guilty of posting deceptive pictures, too. A classic example is a guy who wears a hat in all his photos to conceal that he is balding or bald. (To all the head-hiders out there: did you really think we *weren't* going to find out?) Many women dig bald men; wouldn't *that* be the kind of woman you want to be with? As with so many other characteristics, *own it!*

This isn't just about inconsistency or mild disappointment; you damage both trust as well as a chance for a second date if you simply are not who you represent yourself to be.

That's not to say that you shouldn't put your best photo forward. By all means, wash your hair, put on some make-up, or take an iron to your favorite shirt before donning it for a pic. The best photos for women are shot from above to below, with your eyes raised; it makes them look larger, and looking up is flirtier. If that's not a good look for you, simply look straight at the camera and smile!

Whatever you do, just keep it real. In one of my profile photos on Bumble, I wore no make-up and a parka—not flattering at all.

Yet, it was one of the photos I got the most compliments on. The photograph showed me, with a beautiful glacier in the background. Not only did the photo transmit the natural and gorgeous setting (Argentina), but it also showed me as comfortable in my skin.

You want to be attractive, yes, but authentic as well. Remember, you don't need a hundred dates. Instead, you need to focus on fewer dates with higher quality partners who will be good, long-term potential matches for you. Choose to reveal your true self, not hide it.

High Quality

Make sure your photos are of decent quality, well-lit, and in focus. Smile in at least one or two shots, if not all of them, genuine smiles where people can see your entire face. Make sure your body language is open, too—no crossed arms or angry looks. And although sunglasses are fine for one of your secondary photos, remember that a potential suitor wants to see your eyes.

If you are a woman, wear form-fitting clothes in at least some of your photos that accentuate your physique—things like dresses, skirts, and high heels, rather than the Bermuda shorts and that AC/DC tank top you wear when gardening. However, if the "real" you does not own a dress or high heels, then of course, just rock your sexiest jeans and cutest tee! Unless you are looking for random hook-ups, note that photos that show too much skin, particularly cleavage, may send the wrong message to men.

Guys, if you dress like a slob, we will assume that you are one—a major turnoff. Most men look sexy in a dress shirt or a suit, and men should include at least one of these photos in their mix. And to the men who think sticking their tongues out in pictures is a turn-on: Yes, we get the innuendo. No, it's not funny or sexy. Even if you really are a funny and fun-loving guy, this is better demonstrated in the text portion of your profile, discussed in the next chapter.

Try to avoid selfies, or include only one in the mix and not as your main profile picture. Do not use selfies doctored by Snapchat or other tools either—unless you are a sixteen-year-old, in which case you shouldn't be on dating apps anyway. And no selfies in the car, please; I will find out on our first date whether you drive a Porsche or a Prius.

Pay attention to the overall surroundings where your photos are taken. You don't need five photos of you at a bar or with a drink in your hand unless you are applying to be a bartender or looking for an AA sponsor. It sends the wrong message. Some people take photos in their home or apartment, which is perfectly fine. Just consider the background. I have swiped left on many guys with dark and dated (or worse, filthy and scary) accommodations because of what that said to me about them—accurate or not.

Guys, I believe I speak for all women when I *beg* of you—*please* do *not* post photos of yourself in the gym! You may think you look sexy working out or standing next to weights and gym equipment. Maybe you think a flexed muscle is like Viagra for women. Maybe you think a sweaty face and a sleeveless shirt are appealing. Or maybe you think *Cool, I worked out, I feel pumped, my muscles are tight, there are mirrors here, let me take a photo for Tinder!* Whatever you think, even if you just feel good about yourself after a workout, if you are not a personal trainer or gym owner, keep the workout photos for your own gratification, and use better ones for the ladies you are trying to attract. (A quality match, will be seeing your fit body in all its glory soon enough!)

Similarly, some men post shirtless photos to show off their bodies. While I enjoy a sculpted body as much as the next girl (or guy), if that's the profile photo, or if there is more than one shirtless photo in the bunch, it sends the wrong message. This is especially true if there's minimal text on the profile. It's not a stretch to assume that person is self-absorbed, only interested in women who are similarly fit, only interested in sex, or all of the above!

Secure

If you value your safety and privacy, do not use your Facebook, LinkedIn, Instagram, or other public profile photos. Google reverse image search can connect people to these sites, and your identity can be compromised before you even know if the person on the other side is real. Unfortunately, home addresses are almost always public record in the U.S., particularly if you are a homeowner. Worst-case scenario, a stalker could show up at your home, or even your workplace. Be authentic and truthful, but don't be careless!

Generally, it's best to leave other people out of your photos, both to respect their privacy, and to further protect yours. Plus, it can take too much time and effort for people to guess who you are in a group, and this is about *you* not how you stack up against the other people in a crowd, especially if it makes you look less attractive in comparison. And no, it's not okay to just blur or black out the faces of kids, exes, family, or friends in pictures—it just looks bizarre! If you have kids, disclose that in your profile. But it's not necessary, nor advisable, for thousands of potential suitors (or scammers, for that matter) to "meet" your children before they have even met you.

It may seem that these four photo characteristics (*recent, real, high quality,* and *secure*) may be stating the obvious, but take it from someone who has viewed more online photos than I care to admit: *they matter.* To get more swipes, take the time to make sure your photos are your best!

Your Basic Information

Many people find it difficult to write about themselves or simply don't know where to start. What follows in this chapter and the next is all the guidance you need to come up with a great profile that works.

We'll start with the easy stuff, and you can gradually build up a complete profile. I've included some helpful before and after examples in the next chapter, so you'll know *exactly* what you should and should not do.

<u>Your Height</u>

Always list your real height—not your height in high heels or while riding a unicycle. Why is this important? A 5'6" man may not want a 5'9" woman like me, and vice versa. If you both are fine with that, great—just be truthful! My sister was fine with dating a much shorter man than her (even though he was so short that from afar, he looked like one of her kids!). Just be honest. When you make obvious misrepresentations, you lose credibility right off the bat and most likely create disappointment in the long run.

In my experience, many shorter-than-average guys (say, under 5'8"), do not even list their height on dating apps. I am 5'9" without heels, and my personal preference is taller guys. Once, I agreed to go on a date with a guy whose profile was unusual and extraordinary, but listed his height at 5'8". Because I was so intrigued by him, I didn't let an inch difference stop me from meeting him. When I did, however, he literally reached my chest—with me wearing flats! He was probably 5'5" on a good day. He also had listed his age as forty-nine but was at least ten years older.

I was angry. Without even taking off my coat much less sitting down, I said, "You just wasted my time. I hope you change your profile instead of lying about your height and age and wasting other women's time, too." Then I walked out. To this day, it remains the shortest date I have ever had.

The lesson here is to be honest in your profile and create boundaries around the honesty of others. I gave this man a chance, but he took advantage of it.

Physical Fitness

Most online dating sites will ask you to list something about your body type or fitness level. You don't have to be brutally honest (like disclosing your weight or measurements), but do list your true fitness and activity levels. For instance, I work out daily, so I list that I am "active" or "very active."

While body type and fitness levels can certainly be a factor in physical attraction, they do a more important job by indicating similar interests. Someone who hikes daily in the mountains is active, yes, but they may also appeal to lovers of nature and the outdoors. Conversely, a triathlete is also very active but may not want to start a relationship with someone whose heart rate only gets up playing video games.

Education / Career

Education level is not important to some, but extremely important to others. As with most significant aspects of a person, I recommend listing it, and of course, listing it truthfully. For me, a college education is important as a screening tool for compatibility. I know a high level of education is not always a measure for intelligence—many idiots have graduated from the Ivy Leagues, and many geniuses dropped out of college or did not go at all. For me, it's simply an easy and reliable screening tool when seeking compatibility.

Regardless of your education, at the very least list what you do for a living. Even if you would like to remain anonymous to initial browsers, you can list your general industry or things to describe your career like "marketing management" or "retail."

Some guys write who they are and where they work directly on their profile, making it very easy to verify their information. That's a plus for me; I can easily check out the company website or social profiles to verify the details. While this can certainly make women feel more comfortable towards men, it is much more difficult for women to do this due to safety concerns.

Religion

This was discussed in detail in Chapter 3. It's a question that is going to be asked on most apps. Again, be honest. List your religion *and* how devout you are. If you expect your partner to be devout as well, list that too. This will allow others to swipe left on you when appropriate, and for you to do the same with them.

Children

We've already covered the importance of full disclosure around children. On your basic profile—the information that a potential partner will see right away—list any children and their ages or at least age range, for example, "3 kids 3-10," or if they are now adults. It's also important to disclose whether you have full, joint, or partial custody.

As discussed, if you have absolute requirements like, "I do not want kids," list that as well. Some apps make this relatively easy, where you can just check a box to indicate your status concerning children, such as "do not have but want," or "have and do not want more." If you are open to your partner having kids, whether you have them or not, list that specifically to avoid confusion or assumptions to the contrary that may reduce your swipes.

Extroverted or Introverted

Although most dating apps do not list this as a required answer or a separate category, it is something worth mentioning on your profile. I know, for example, that I am an extrovert and that I generally get along better with other extroverts. I do have good friends who are introverts, and I could potentially date one, but someone who is highly introverted, would likely not be the best match.

If you know that you are *extremely* introverted or extroverted, it's even more important to put it out there. That doesn't mean that opposites cannot attract—they often do—but extremes in any area can make for difficult matches.

You're not just looking for similar character traits in a partner, but those that complement yours as well. Remember my example of easygoing versus high maintenance? I would like my partner to be easygoing because I most certainly am not! It would just be too much for our relationship if both of us were at the same end of the scale.

Zodiac Sign

For the majority of people, a zodiac sign is not important. But some apps do ask for it, and some people voluntarily list it even when it's not required. There are a handful of people who would not date someone with an incompatible sign. Other people don't care. Some refuse to list their zodiac sign even when asked.

My take? If you find someone who seems compatible, go with it, regardless of their sign. But if you are deeply invested in astrology, definitely list your sign as well as the one(s) you are seeking.

* * *

Building a high-quality profile can seem complicated or intimidating. If you're feeling discouraged, just take it one step at a time—your careful preparation in Chapters 1 through 5 will help.

Once you have your basics established, move on to the next chapter. In it, you'll learn some of the more advanced aspects of building your profile, including how to add unique descriptors to hook the partner you want!

CHAPTER 7

Your Profile 2.0

Be yourself; everyone else is already taken.

—Oscar Wilde

Based on your work in the previous chapter, how do you *look*? Would you swipe right on yourself based only on your basic profile?

Many potential partners will swipe one way or the other based strictly on your primary photo, but that doesn't mean you should neglect how you present yourself in words. This is far trickier than you might imagine, but fear not! While there are many variables, you have to do your best to account for all of them. This chapter is designed to help you navigate this complexity with ease. What follows will give you all the information you need, without all the painful trial and error that most people experience.

Dating is Marketing

In business, marketing is about matching between the company and consumers—the company is trying to connect with customers that are a good fit for its product or service. Dating is no different. But instead of a traditional advertisement, your job is to create an online profile that can do the same thing—connect you with good matches.

Like a business, a great profile creates a funnel of potential good "leads" or matches. You filter them through your pre-qualifying funnel criteria (remember all that inner work you did earlier?), and make dating choices.

If a company doesn't capture leads, or those leads are a bad fit, sales don't happen. In dating, if you don't capture leads, or the leads you do get don't match, then quality *relationships* don't happen.

Your profile is what creates the large funnel of leads. Filling out your profile description and uploading quality and unique photos is a significant step. Your quality photos attract the leads, and your detailed text description weed out many suitors who won't be quality matches for you.

Dating, especially online, is a process of elimination. The goal is for you to end up with fewer leads or matches down the funnel that will be good potential matches with all the criteria you have set up. Just like a salesperson doesn't want to spend hours selling a product to someone who will never be happy with it, you don't want to spend hours on dates with people who will never match.

There is an illusion of choice in online dating. It feels like there are a limitless number of potential matches because there are so many people using the apps at any given time. In reality, however, based on who you are (your age group, etc.) and who your potential match *needs* to be, the pool is smaller than it seems. There are certainly enough potential matches out there for you, but they are not infinite in number. You want to reserve your time and energy for those who could be good potential matches for you and weed out the others early on.

The goal, then, is to build your profile in a way that is targeted, specific, and that appeals to the kind of person you want to attract. And yes, as with marketing, you also want to include a strong "call to action." A generic profile can be easily overlooked by the right person, who has likely seen dozens or hundreds of similarly unpolished profiles. In my experience, there are *so* many men's profiles that all look like they belong to the same guy—who, by the way, is one I don't want to date. But if you craft your profile carefully, you can appeal directly to a likely match and pretty much bet on a swipe right.

No matter which website or app you may be using for online dating, the process that follows will work. Each website or app has different profile tools and a unique look and feel, but the principles of being specific and taking the time to do the job right still apply. Follow the steps and tools that the app provides you, but keep the substance the same. You can use the same profile across multiple websites and apps. Some have a character limit, whereas others require you to fill out questionnaires; regardless, taking the time to work through the steps ahead will be helpful across all platforms.

Choosing Your Dating App / Website

Note that you will get different results on different apps. With *eHarmony*, I spent a ton of time filling out their detailed questionnaire, and yet I could not find *one* man who was enough of a fit with me for a date in my entire ninety-day trial.

My recommendation? Play around with various websites and apps until you are comfortable with a select few. *Tinder,* that was once pretty much just a "hook-up" app only, has reinvented itself as the most widely used dating app both for hook-ups and serious daters. *Bumble* is a favorite of mine. *OkCupid* was not great for me, but like *Tinder* and *Bumble,* it's free to use, as is *PlentyOfFish,* another very popular site. They also have useful paid upgrade options that allow you to save time by seeing who liked you first, leaving you fewer people to filter.

Both *Match* and *eHarmony* are popular as well, but they do require a paid subscription. In all cases, if you are serious about dating, I recommend paying for the subscription. Free versions have limited options, and more important, *you're worth it.*

Some apps are also better than others depending on your locale. Ask your single friends which are best and then simply sign up for two or three. (Too many apps will be difficult to stay on top of, but two or three are manageable.)

Creating Your Detailed Profile

Both men and women who write complete profiles or bios receive substantially more swipes or matches than people who do not have descriptions, or have only minimal ones. To help you with this vital profile-building skill, I'll discuss in detail each section with examples first and then build a complete profile at the end to combine all the parts.

After your choice of photos, checked boxes, and blanks are filled in, next comes the text—the description of who you are and what's unique about you.

Many people find this the most difficult part, but stick with it. A good profile will increase your chances to receive *quality* leads, filtering out the initial matches who just liked your photos or found you attractive.

I recommend that you write your initial profile on a tablet computer, or smartphone. You'll save a lot of time by being able to edit and copy and paste later into your chosen website or app. Make sure to use spellcheck too—poor grammar and typos might be a turnoff to some quality partners. Remember, the effort and care you put into your profile now will be reflected in the quality of the matches you find!

Let's do this!

Build Yourself Up!

It's imperative that you build a non-generic profile—one that uniquely describes *you*. You know who you really are and what your best attributes and characteristics are from the lists you prepared. All that hard work in early chapters starts paying off now!

Be sure to write about yourself in the best positive light, and avoid negativity and put-downs. Low self-esteem is a big turn-off for many quality men and women. Even if you are only joking, there is a higher likelihood someone will just swipe right (well, left, really) past you; humor doesn't translate well in short profiles.

Make sure you write something *worthwhile* on your profile, too, rather than just completing the minimum categories (like height and education). The biggest reason I swipe away from men, even those I find attractive, is either no text or just a bare minimum description, such as *likes to go out to movies and concerts*. People who do not write anything on their profiles aren't serious about a long-term relationship; they aren't revealing anything about themselves or what they are seeking in a partner. If someone can't make a ten-minute effort to write something interesting about himself on his profile, he's not worth one minute of my time or yours—keep on swiping!

My advice for men who want to get more matches is to put an interesting text description that includes unique information about them, in addition to putting up good photos (described in the previous chapter). Women, although men may use photos as their first filter, the same rules apply to you. Do *not* short-change your written profile.

If your description is interesting, hopefully even intriguing, and your photos are attractive enough, then you *will* get likes or swipes regardless. Put yourself in the best light possible, including complimenting yourself. Think of how your best friend would describe you, and use the same language—don't hold back. Be positive and not critical. There's no need for you to present anything less than a flattering view of yourself. Would you date someone with a profile saying: *I hate the way I look. I need to lose 20 lbs*?

This is *not* lying—you need to be pragmatic. Too many of us are self-critical, but this isn't the time or place for it. Do you want to stay home feeling sorry for yourself, or go on a hot date? In marketing terms, you need to build a sufficiently large funnel and then screen or weed your leads to lead yourself to potential first dates—what marketers call "conversions." Put differently, you need to cast a wide net to catch as many fish as you can, and then select the ones that might be keepers!

Unlike the marketing world, however, your "conversion rate" doesn't matter. You don't need to have hundreds or thousands of potential partners—just enough quality matches for you to take to the next step. Remember that swipe rates are generally low, especially for men. Keep your profile interesting and let your personality shine. You want to portray yourself as exciting, fun, intelligent, and unique.

One of the funniest and well-written profiles I came across included: *My dream dinner guests are Franklin Roosevelt (alive, not now), Robin Williams (also preferably alive).* He was funny and witty throughout his profile and I immediately agreed to a date to get to know him better. In person, he was indeed funny, brilliant, and memorable. That connection only happened because he invested the time in his written profile.

The main blunder most people make when they begin building their profile (other than not writing anything at all), is that it's too generic and therefore uninteresting. A general statement like "any questions just ask" is *not* a good example as it does not invite any person to waste time asking questions. Be special. Be memorable. Be unique. Don't try to be everything to all people—it won't work. You want to attract a specific type of person, so write your profile so that it will be attractive to *them and no one else.*

Here are a few examples of how nuances can help you escape the generic profile pitfall. Many men write: *I love being outdoors.* On the surface, that may seem like a helpful thing to include on a profile. But think of the wide variety of activities and interests that statement could include: fishing, water skiing, riding in a convertible with the top down, cooking hot dogs over a fire and drinking beer, gardening, hunting, going to the beach, jogging, outdoor concerts, tent camping, white water rafting—the list is almost endless!

Each combination, of course, can also represent a different type of guy. Is a dedicated hunter who loves country music and sleeping outdoors the same as a collector of convertible cars who loves to drive to jazz festivals with the top down?

A lover of the outdoors would be much better to list something specific like:

I love deep sea fishing in the summer, snow skiing at Lake Tahoe in the winter, and on any nice evening, watching the sun set from my back porch listening to James Taylor.

Or instead of *I enjoy cooking,* you could say:

I enjoy cooking healthy meals for my family and friends. My favorites are lasagna and home-made pasta with a great bottle of Chianti.

See what a difference specifics can make? In each case, the nuanced profile helps to identify and attract the *right* quality partner by giving them enough information to know that they should swipe right.

Another good tip is to use humor and wit if you can, provided it doesn't make you feel awkward. Humor can be tricky to pull off in a short online profile. I wrote on my profile: *My mother would describe me as "the best thing that happened to the universe!"* While it is clearly a joke—making fun of both myself and my mother—it also lets someone know I am not lacking in self-confidence. The right guy would pick up on (and appreciate) the sarcasm, as well as my comfort in my own skin.

Identify Your Desired Partner

Now it's time to shift from your best qualities, to those of a potential partner. The list you made earlier of the top qualities and characteristics that you hope to find will help. Once again, your hard work at the preparation stage is paying off!

If you struggle to get started, here's an easy-to-follow template:

I'm looking for a _____ (best quality that describes

your desired partner), _____ *(second best quality that describes your desired partner), and* _____ *(third best quality that describes your desired partner) to share* _____ *(activity #1),* _____ *(activity #2), and* _____ *(activity #3) together.*

If you refer to your lists in Chapter 4, you'll find this to be a quick and easy task! Space permitting, you can also add what kind of relationship you want. Some people write *LTR* for long-term relationship, or *nothing serious, friends with benefits,* etc., all of which are good (when truthful, of course) because they serve to screen out those who don't fit.

Profile descriptors such as *I don't know yet* simply lack clarity, something you should have in abundance by now. The reason most dates don't work is that so many people either haven't bothered to figure out what they really want, or are not focusing exclusively on it. It is much easier to hit a bullseye if you know where it is and aim directly for it!

Furthermore, steer clear of desperate statements like, *I am looking for the right man to complete me,* or, *I need a woman who will support me in every way.* Such remarks are insulting to you, and make you appear needy and insecure. If you truly feel that way, you just are not *appearing* needy and insecure; you *are.* In that event, please return to Chapters 2 and 3 and have another in-depth work on yourself again! Similarly, I have seen profiles before that read: *If you do not return calls, if you want to text for five days and then ghost me, swipe left.* This type of language only transmits that the woman is bitter, demanding, and clingy—all major turn-offs. Self-confidence and happiness are two character traits that attract the best kind of partner.

Finally, it's not yet the time to disclose your "do-not-wish" or even "hate" lists here; hold them back for the next screening steps. For one, you'll waste valuable space, which is limited on many apps. More important, you do not want to give away your deal-breaker list ahead of time—instead, you'll want to protect yourself from people who may not be honest with you. In my experience, most people in the dating world fib a little, and many lie outright. If a man finds you attractive, and you state up front that you cannot stand a man who is a slob, he very well may lie about that in order to meet (or sleep with) you, and hide it from you until ... you walk into The Dog Guy's house!

The screening steps in the next chapters will include you "interviewing" the other person and asking questions that will help you determine if they share your values and beliefs. You do not want to give away the answers.

Before and After Profiles

The following are examples of poorly written profiles and how they could be rewritten to be more appealing. None of these are exaggeration—they all come from my experience in the world of dating. (Trust me, it's far better to learn from them here than from real-world experience!)

Bad example: *I am an open book. Just ask.*

This tells me nothing. At best, it indicates disinterest in a truly meaningful relationship. At worst, in my experience, once you actually *do* start asking hard questions, these "open book" folks slam shut.

Rewrite: *I am a published research scientist working for the CDC to prevent diseases from spreading. I am loyal, honest, and affectionate. I love tech toys, assembling things, and figuring out how things* *work. I am looking for a LTR with a woman who is intelligent, confident, easy-going and who likes sci-fi movies and novels, staying at home, and watching Netflix.*

Bad example: *I just moved to the area. I would like to meet someone.*

Again, this does not give any specific information about the person. In fact, you can't tell if they are genuinely new to the "area" (what area would that be?), or someone oceans away looking to catfish their next victim. I need details to ascertain that you are truly someone new in the neighborhood.

Rewrite: *I just moved to Atlanta for a new marketing job. I am adventurous, funny as hell, and gregarious (but not the obnoxious variety). I would like to meet a woman, preferably in her thirties without children, so we could start a family together. I am a wine connoisseur and have actually traveled to both the Napa and Sonoma Valleys as well as France to visit vineyards. Looking for an intelligent, independent, and successful woman with a similar passion for wine and travel, and for my badass sense of humor.*

Bad example: *I have recently come into a lot of money, and I want to travel and explore new places and settle down and spoil the one I am with.*

One would think or hope that no one would be naïve enough to disclose such a thing. (Then again, one would think no one would post nude pictures either, right?) Obviously, this is going to attract the gold-diggers, those who are looking for sugar daddies and monetary compensation for companionship and sex. (There are other websites out there for those who want that.) But if you're looking for something genuine, you aren't going to find it with that kind of profile.

Rewrite: *I am a generous, loving, and caring partner who loves* to cook, especially Italian food. I enjoy international travel, trips to the beach, and volunteering at a soup kitchen. I would like to travel the world with a fun, creative, and free-spirited woman without kids at home to experience climbing mountains, walks in nature, learning about new cultures and languages, experiencing new foods, and everything else in between that the world has to offer.

Bad example: *I am the mother of two grown children who are out of the house. One is married with no children. The other has a daughter and another daughter on the way.*

This gives no information about the woman herself, other than she has two grown children. Does a man who wants to date this woman care about her grown children and whether they are married or not? No, he wants to date *her*, not her children. Worse, the only real information she gave is that she's a grandmother! She may be only in her forties, but she's made herself sound much older. These details can come later, after they meet. But with so many men looking for youth, or at least youthfulness, they don't want to hear "Granny!" in the back of their minds when they look at your profile pictures.

Rewrite: *Funny, creative, and empathetic sales professional, mother to two girls, both have flown the nest. I enjoy spending time with family, making homemade pizza and grilling out, going to the lake, and listening to pop music and concerts (Taylor Swift, Katy Perry). Looking for a man with older children who is smart, analytical, and can make me belly laugh.*

Bad example: *Broke up with my boyfriend recently. Time to move on.*

This makes this person seem like a potential liability at best. Why is she still discussing her break-up if she's gotten over it and ready to move on? Moreover, if the break-up was recent, why is she already looking for someone new? This profile gives the impression that she is either not an invested partner or looking for a rebound. No man in search of a meaningful relationship would match with a profile like that. Instead, it only invites "players" to ask this woman out because they assume she'll be an easy target on the rebound.

Rewrite: No rewrite needed here. What this woman really needs is to read Chapter 2 to find out if she's really ready and work on herself!

Here are a few more well-written profiles I have helped create:

I'm a 35YO Latina divorced mother of 4 children—3 teenage boys and a 3-year-old princess—all who live with me. I work in the real estate field. I enjoy going to the beach every chance I get, and love getting my feet sandy or cooking fish (that you have caught and cleaned)! I'm looking for a mature, confident, and caring man who will remember my birthday and pick me flowers even if it's just from the side of the road. Family is everything to me, so it's very important that you also have children or understand that my kids are my priority.

* * *

I'm a historian who teaches at a university, so I'm a total nerd who spends half his day buried in books. Love discussing academic ideas and theories, then following up on them with research. Looking for a fellow academic who can indulge in this pleasure with me.

* * *

I'm an intelligent, successful, and passionate buyer in the fashion industry with an international background and clientele. I love art, traveling to international destinations (Vancouver, Berlin, China), or the beach (Bermuda, Caribbean), exploring adventures, tennis, animals, spending time with friends and family, bourbon, wine, and fine dining. Two girls 18 and 16. I enjoy witty humor. Hoping you can make me laugh and teach me something new. LTR only.

App Q&A

Some apps have categories you can add to help better describe yourself. They are generally referred to as "profile prompts," and can be good ice breakers, as well as a way to make your profile unique and compelling. As a bonus, these prompts give you more room to describe yourself, which is always helpful. I highly recommend filling out at least a few.

Here are a few examples:

Favorite quality in a person...

I feel most empowered when...

We'll get along if....

My mother would describe me as ...

After work, you can find me...

If I could teleport to anywhere this weekend, it would be....

Two truths and a lie...

Beach or Mountains...

I would skip this one unless you are really passionate about one of them, and then you need to list why. For example: *Beach, because I love the fresh seafood, the smell of the salt air, and the sound of the waves crashing, particularly at night.*

Nightclub or Netflix...

I would skip this question, too, and choose something more personal and informational, or at the very least (if you select *Netflix*), include examples of what kinds of shows you enjoy watching, like *Game of Thrones.*

If I could donate a million dollars, it would be to...

For this one, please don't write stupid answers, like this one: *Myself, duh, I want to be rich.* (Okay, maybe that was mildly amusing, and probably truthful, but still, it's not helping find a match.)

* * *

Now that you finished writing, editing, and possibly re-writing your profile, review it in its entirety again to make sure there are no spelling mistakes, and that the profile is consistent with your photos. Does your description match the photos? Do you look genuine, act your age, and convey the message you want?

Remember that none of this is set in stone. You can always change it later if you decide you don't like it or if you aren't getting many swipes.

Are you excited? You *should* be! You are now "out there," ready to get right-swipes, likes, hearts, and more!

Next, it's time to move on to screening all those matches to find the best one for you!

CHAPTER 8

Screening

Luck is what happens when preparation meets opportunity.

–Seneca

If you're new to online dating, you may be surprised to discover that there are indeed plenty of fish in the sea. In a year and a half of dating, I received over 10,000 likes or right-swipes. My "slow" days were ten or so. On some days, I received over a hundred.

To be clear, women definitely have the upper hand when it comes to this early stage interest—they get significantly more swipes than men. But that upper hand, as crazy as it may sound, can be a burden. There may be plenty of fish in the sea, but most of them, it turns out, need to be thrown back. And that takes time and effort.

As a busy professional, I don't have the time to go over the dozens, much less hundreds of profiles of men who right-swipe me. I already have a demanding career, a daughter, and a full social life. I don't need another exhaustive task on my plate.

To save myself the effort (and keep my sanity), I had to develop a system to screen potential men quickly and effectively. I needed the best way possible to get rid of the men who would never be a match without accidentally missing the ones who might.

In this chapter, I'll teach you, regardless of your gender, how to do the same: to weed your garden to let the most beautiful flowers grow. Like flowers, there is only so much space and time, and the best ones need both to flourish! This chapter will focus on screening your potential matches before deciding to meet a person in real life.

Before we begin, let's quickly revisit your lists from the previous chapters, specifically your partner *must*, *wish*, and *do-not-wish* lists. Keep those lists top of mind, or even in hard copy next to you when you go through the profiles of potential matches.

***

If you've ever read a marketing or sales book, you'll know many of the principles that follow. For the benefit of those who may not be familiar with sales and marketing concepts, let's discuss some screening basics.

To attract new customers to a business, the marketing department first builds a *funnel*. This means using advertising to cast a wide net over many potential customers. When the marketing team gets a lead (someone responds to the ad), they are put into the top, or wide end, of the funnel.

The funnel is a list of questions, processes, or qualifiers that help to determine if potential customers are the right fit for the business and its product or service. For example, if you are a retailer like Bloomingdale's that sells to high-end customers, the funnel tries to determine, either directly or indirectly, the potential customer's disposable income. Someone making minimum wage isn't Bloomingdale's target market, so the business *wants* to disqualify them early on in the process instead of investing time, money, and effort trying to sell to them. The minimum wage demographic mostly likely won't choose to shop at Bloomingdale's, and the sooner the business learns this, the better.

Dating is similar. Initially, you want to cast a wide net across as many potential partners as possible, and then screen for quality matches through a funnel that you create. This funnel will weed people out based on *your* criteria of who is a good match, and you will *only* go on actual in-person dates with those who make it through *your* funnel.

Don't underestimate this screening process. Dating people who aren't a match does more than just waste your time—every date you have with someone who you will never fit with is a missed opportunity to date someone who *could*.

Initial Screening

Photos
The first screening step is both simple and purely visual: just look at their photos. Because there are so many people to screen, this is by far the quickest and easiest way forward.

I look at the photos, sometimes even just the profile photo, and reject anyone who I know there is no chance I would ever be attracted to. It may seem harsh as some people may not be photogenic, and sometimes I was pleasantly surprised when my dates looked better in person than in their photos.

But, don't feel bad about initial screening based on physical characteristics; this is not a "find my bestie" endeavor! We all have our unique taste—follow your gut and don't waste unnecessary time and energy on anyone who will never attract you. If you're unsure about some, keep them for a second round of screening. After some practice, they will all be quick and easy rejections. I now do this in a split-second, with no need to look at a photo more than once. That is not to say that if you have a moment of pause looking at a main photo, and if someone has multiple photos, you should not go ahead and look at the rest of them. But after that, it should be an easy left or right swipe.

I also swipe away from men who don't post photos with full head and body shots, photos with only sunglasses, photos that are out of focus or too dark, profiles that only have one or two photos, or profiles where most photos are from a distance or with other people.

Likewise, I swipe away from photos where I don't like the environment—like the previously mentioned nasty bathroom selfie, or a home where I would never want to spend time in *any* room. Furthermore, I swipe away from profiles with fake smiles or those without a single photo of the person smiling. And of course, anything that comes close to a dick pic is a deal-breaker—guys, no woman is interested in looking at your junk online.

Luke was a sweet guy who, based on his profile, appeared to be intelligent and unique. From his photos, I felt that he wasn't my type, but I thought, "You never know." (Spoiler alert: most of the time you do.)

Our text conversations were funny and clever, and we decided to meet in person for coffee. We connected on an intellectual and personality level right away. He was a bright, nice, and authentic guy, easy-going and independent, with a great sense of humor. The problem was that I just wasn't attracted to him and never would be. For all his positive attributes, I couldn't imagine myself ever kissing him. In retrospect, I shouldn't have wasted my time or his by meeting in person. The only reason I did was that he met *most* of my screening criteria, and I thought he might be more attractive to me in person. He wasn't.

There were other times when I wasn't sure about my attraction on the first date, so I went on a second date because I thought the men were good potential matches. I learned quickly that if I'm not attracted to someone on the first date, I most likely am not going to be attracted to them on the second or third date, either. Some people are different, however, and can develop attraction over time. That hasn't been the case with me.

The lesson is this: at this "photos-only" stage, if you think there is even a *possibility* of attraction, go to the next screening phase (the written profile).

Before we move on, let me give you a quick word of warning about profile photos. If they appear too professional or too "perfect" or raise your eyebrow for any reason, you would be wise to do a quick check. In Google Chrome, simply right-click on the image and select "Search Google for image." On your smartphone, just tap and hold the photo, and then click the same feature. If you are not using Google Chrome, there are other options for this. Just "Google" it (pun intended!). You'll be shown any other online locations where the photo appears.

If all of the profile photos were taken exclusively for the dating app, nothing will pop up. Any photos that do appear may help you determine if the person is legitimate—you might find the photo on social media or corporate sites, for example. Or, you may learn that their profile photos are fake—pulled from someone else's social posts, or even perhaps from a Calvin Klein ad from years past of a gorgeous Italian model. This is one of the many benefits of modern technology; use it!

Written Profile

The second screening step involves carefully reading a potential match's written profile. Remember, this isn't a competition to get as many first dates as possible. Likewise, people (ladies!), this process is not about getting free drinks or dinners. Your goal is to identify who is *worthy* of a first date, not who is *willing*. Your time is more valuable than that, as is everyone else's. I have heard many stories from men about women they suspected went on a date with them just to get a free meal. Be a decent human being—don't use people this way. Instead, remember your earlier work. Make a point to read written profiles with an eye for *matching*, not simply meeting.

During my online dating experiences, I've seen more than a few weird profiles. A guy named Oliver's read: *I absolutely loathe pickles.* That was it. Huh? Even if I had found it amusing (which I did not), why would he only write that out of all the things he could write in that space? Was he trying to disqualify the overwhelming tide of pickle-loving ladies?

Another, Hector, wrote, *I love sex,* and that his dream dinner guest was *pizza.* At least he was honest about the sex, although my guess is the only action he got with his pizza date was indigestion. Yet another, Rick, wrote: *'I have a high sex drive, but I don't fuck anything that walks.'* Thank you, Rick, for making my screening job so much easier.

Brian's main profile picture was of a wolf (first indicator to left-swipe). Not even a human being, but a *wolf.* And he wrote, '*A gentleman is simply a patient wolf.*' What? That sounded a little too *Silence of the Lamb*s for me. Another man, "Stoney," did use his own photo, and wrote, '*Looking for smoke buddies.*' To his credit, he was at least honest.

Another swiper, Sam, didn't fill out any important information beyond *male looking for female,* and simply wrote, *'I just joined, will fill this out later.'* Bob wrote that if he could solve one world problem, it would be, *'Letting the world know how cool I am.'* (Not cool, Bob! I suspect this may not be a global issue, but a problem just a little closer to home.) Or how about Tom, who wrote, *'I'm not easy. I've been called batshit crazy by people who know me.'* Well, Tom, I don't know you, but I think you *are* batshit crazy for putting that on *Bumble*!

You should find these profiles off-putting, and they should also illustrate how important it is to *read* the profile. None of these men are serious about finding a long-term partner. If they were, they'd spend a few minutes sharing some real personal details. Lack of seriousness is the best case scenario—people who provide minimal information may be trying to be deceptive, manipulative, or hide their true selves. Either way, don't waste time asking twenty questions via app texting just to find out. If their profile provides little or no information or is simply bizarre or creepy, swipe away and move on.

Another red flag is a written profile that seems inconsistent with the photos or basic profile information like education, interests, locale, etc. For example, would a person claiming to be a highly-educated professional have a written profile full of misspellings and poor grammar? The problem isn't the writing mistakes, it's that something about this particular fish in the sea doesn't smell quite right. It's a red flag. (More on this ahead.)

Based on *your* preferences, there are other incompatibilities that make for easy screening. Armed with your *must, wish,* and *do-not-wish* lists, swiping left or right becomes so much faster and easier. You want to have kids, and the profile makes it clear that the prospective suitor does not? Easy swipe away. They "love Jesus" and you are an atheist? The same. You are 5'6" and will not date a woman taller than you, and she is 5'11"? Swipe on.

Deeper Screening

Good news: the previous quick and easy screening steps will weed out the vast majority of people. You're now that much further down the funnel!

Next, we progress to the exciting arena of dating Q&A, wherein you begin asking questions of potential partners and answering theirs. Again, our goal is to waste neither your time nor your energy on potential dates that go nowhere.

This deeper screening stage involves messaging within a dating app to get more information on those potential matches who have "survived" your initial screening. Let's be clear: by messaging, I do not mean *hi*, a smiley face, a heart, or a thumbs-up. Far too many people (in particular men, in my experience) consider a right-swipe or like to be their initial "message." It isn't, and it gets a suitably terrible response rate. Similarly, if someone (guys, I'm talking about you again, but we ladies love you!) only messages the grossly over-used *Hey Sexy* or *Hello Gorgeous*, don't fall into the newbie trap of thinking, *Awww, they think I'm beautiful!*

Um, girl ... *no.* You should assume that person put *zero* effort into reading your profile or coming up with an original way to start a conversation. Don't flatter yourself; they *do* say this to *all* the girls! They're using the shotgun approach to get you to bed, rather than aiming for the bullseye of a lasting match with a quality person like you!

Deeper Screening Questions

Before you start with more in-depth screening, it's helpful to take the time to create a list of screening questions. Fortunately, this is an easy job now that you've gone through the mental exercises and list-making of earlier chapters.

Remember that your goal here is *screening*. You want to weed out the catfishers, liars, and fake profiles, as well as those who simply don't meet the criteria you have already established.

But won't I have fewer dates?

Yes.

At the beginning of this book, you may have assumed that the goal is to go on as many dates as possible—a kind of random, needle-in-a-haystack search for your dream relationship.

By now, it should be clear that the actual goal is *fewer* dates, not more. Rather than randomly shooting into the air hoping to hit *something*, your job is to keep your eye on *your* bullseye. Will your screening lead to fewer dates? Yes. Will they be dates of greater potential that can lead you to a lasting match? Absolutely!

Your screening questions are meant to understand the other person and screen them according to your likes and dislikes. *Screening puts you in control of your destiny.* Very good starter questions, asked of someone you have "matched" with after the initial screening, are specific to their profile, or yours. *What did you like about my profile* is a good one to ask, particularly of men, who have a tendency not to read profiles. If he answers this question with sufficient detail, either he read your profile, or at least took the time to do so after you messaged.

If you wrote that you love gardening, and he says, *Well, in addition to your dimples (which are pretty cute, BTW), I am so happy to see a girl who doesn't mind getting her hands dirty!* Then you know he has read your profile and appears interested in getting to know more about you.

Similarly, for a higher response rate, take a look at the other person's profile, and ask an interesting question that relates to something they wrote. For example, if someone has said they enjoy skydiving, you might write, *Well, I have never felt the urge to jump out of a perfectly functioning airplane, but perhaps you could make me see the fun in it?! Care to share?* Or if someone says they like to cook, ask: *Since you love to cook, why don't you send me your all-time favorite recipe? I will reciprocate!* These tailored messages are much more likely to entice the other person to reply and start a conversation. Notice each of these ends with an open question to make it easier for the other person to respond.

After you've started up a conversation, good ol' common sense and your unique personality come into play. I can't script messages for you—just be yourself (but cautiously, particularly at first). Once your message conversation begins, you will immediately begin to learn much about the other person. In addition to what you have already learned from their written profile, you should be able to begin to glean things such as:

- responsive (or not)
- good or poor grammar
- intelligent (or not)
- a fake / fraud / catfisher / scammer / liar / con artist
- sense of humor (or lack thereof)
- confidence and self-esteem (or lack thereof)
- interests, in addition to any already listed
- self-centeredness

- level of education
- a player or interested in sex only
- other issues (angry responses, bizarre behavior, etc.)

Most of these are not intended to imply "good" or "bad" (well, except the obvious ones – like LIAR! or SCAM ARTIST!) We are all unique, with our own individual tastes and interests, likes and dislikes, "musts" and "hates" … so as you send and receive messages, keep your handy-dandy lists in the back of your mind, if not even right in front of you!

You are now officially in the deep end, with no floaties needed! Much of what happens now comes from your common sense and individuality. Before you start swimming, however, let me share some potential red flags and pitfalls that I have learned through painful experience.

Red Flags

I assume that if you bought this book, you probably aren't looking for friends with benefits, one-night stands, or no-strings-attached sex. Historically, those are pretty easy to come by without the aid of a book!

In a perfect world, if hook-ups are an online dater's primary purpose for being on an app, they will have been relatively candid about this on their profile. Nevertheless, you should be able to pick up on that very quickly during this deeper screening process. Typically, these people will instantly send flirty, suggestive, or downright dirty messages. And if you respond in kind, they will want to get your phone number with lightning speed and arrange a "meeting" (hook-up) right away. They will also be much more prone to send you photos, which inevitably will include risqué (or partial or fully naked) pictures and a request for reciprocation.

If casual sex is what you want, good news, this is probably the easiest thing to identify early on in your screening. If it isn't, remember to concentrate on your *why*. Consider your lists (wish, not-wish, deal-breakers) and keep your eyes on the real prize. Many men write on their profiles that they are looking for a long-term relationship or that they are looking for friends and open for more with the right woman or something of the sort and then want to meet you immediately before they asked you real questions to get to know you.

Next, on to a universal red flag. If someone's photos and written profile all look good, but the messaging seems "off," it probably is. For example, if the written profile is one way (fairly articulate, perhaps), but when they are forced to communicate "live" with you, it seems completely different, this is likely not a good sign. The most likely culprit is that they are *not* the person in their photos, but a catfisher, probably located in another country, communicating with you for less-than-honorable reasons.

If you are suspicious, but not ready to rule them out yet, ask some "innocent" questions about where they say they live, but don't give them long to answer. If you live in Austin, Texas, and they claim to as well, ask them something fairly specific or unique about Austin, preferably something they cannot quickly Google. Or ask very specific questions about the part of town they live or work in. Where did they go to school? What is their favorite restaurant, or park, or music venue?

Another red flag—always, always, *always*—is if they are claiming to be a U.S. native, but their English is not that of a U.S. native English speaker. (For the record, this isn't about weeding out non-U.S.

natives. I *am* a non-U.S. native with excellent English.)

In that vein, if someone seems too quickly or overly curious about what you do for a living, your level of income, or your financial circumstances, *block them and move on!* You would be amazed at how many people are hit up within the first few days, and sometimes even sooner for "emergency" funds to pay for outrageous (and fraudulent) expenses. If they start giving you a sob story, don't even wait for the request. BLOCK!

Another obvious red flag is someone who is married and lying about it. This can become apparent in multiple ways. This includes profile photos without a full face-shot, generally being "squirrely" about communication, particularly only during certain times of the day or nonsensical requests that you do not text or call; later on, wanting to meet in very private places, etc.

Remember that just because someone is cautious (as you should be), doesn't mean they're lying. For example, you may want to exchange phone numbers with someone relatively quickly, and they may resist. But obviously, exchanging numbers too soon can have both pros and cons. The drawbacks are relatively obvious: they have your phone number, and can most likely discover your identity, including potentially where you live and work, whether you've been arrested before, and more. The advantages are relatively obvious as well: you have their phone number, and can most likely discover their identity, including potentially where they live and work, whether they have been arrested before, and more. It's a double-edged sword.

Similarly, if someone is clearly avoiding revealing their true identity after a little while (including their last name, where they work, or other personal information), this could indicate untruthfulness because they are lying, scamming, catfishing, or married. But it could also represent nothing more than caution. And although you might assume that primarily women would want to be safety-conscious, women can be "scary," too. (Remember *Fatal Attraction*?)

Again, the best advice here is to keep your radar on and use common sense. Before you actually meet for a first date, you'll do an even deeper level of screening—more on that ahead.

One way to maintain privacy or anonymity while still in the deeper screening stage is to get a different phone number through services such as Google Voice or Hushed for a small fee. There are also free apps such as TextNow and Talkatone that you can use for texts as well as voice calls, as long as you have WiFi. Don't despair if someone gives you a phone number that does not "check out." They may be doing the same thing *you* are: just being cautious.

Deeper Deeper Screening

If a potential match passes the earlier smell tests and after some initial contact you continue to find them interesting and attractive (and not yet exhibiting any of your *hate* or *do-not-wish* attributes or behaviors), then you can quickly move on to what I refer to as deeper deeper screening questions.

If there's no potential fit for your personal *why* or any other deal-breakers, *do not* waste your time or theirs. It doesn't matter how physically attractive someone is, how entertaining their messaging is, or how much money they make; unless they check all of your *must* boxes, quite a few of your *wish* boxes, and absolutely none of your *hates*, move on.

At this point in the funnel, it's time to ask any unanswered questions you have. For example, if you know that a potential match has young children, and particularly if you do as well, you should ask fairly quickly about custody arrangements and schedules. As discussed, this can dramatically impact quality time with this person. Likewise, if your faith is extremely important to you or in a partner, and they have neglected to mention it, now is the time to ask.

Prior to a first date, you should have answers to every *must, hate, must not* issue, as well as most of your *wish* and *do-not-wish* items. Do *not* hint at the answers you're looking for or give them any clues. Your job is to find out who they are, not to fool yourself into believing they're someone else, or worse, let them manipulate you with the answers you want to hear. There is no need to dance around the questions. Just get out your lists, and using your unique style, simply ask!

As you continue to message with a potential match, you'll also be learning a lot about their personality and behavior. For example, you should be able to determine fairly quickly if they only want to talk about themselves, rather than learning about you as well. You'll also be able to pick up on things like intelligence, sense of humor, outlook on life, background, and opinions. A thoughtful suitor will also be making the same assessments of *you*!

Pay attention to how frequently (or infrequently) someone communicates with you, and the possible reasons. Some people may message or call less frequently because they have very demanding jobs, or, it may just be their style. They may be insecure or passive or shy. You have to assess your own needs and tolerance level, so file these things away, too.

Personal preference aside, pursuing someone in today's world follows a pattern. It starts with swiping, then messaging via an app. It progresses to texting after phone numbers are exchanged, then calling, and then finally, an in-person date. Each exchange is different, but you can learn a lot from how things proceed. If someone messages you several times a day at first, and then you don't hear from them for a few days, the odds are *not* that they had a terrible car accident and are in a coma, but that they lost interest. Conversely, if they text you once every other day, and then progress to texting and calling multiple times a day, a first date is probably on the horizon!

Pulling the Plug

There will be times, of course, when you progress to deeper (or a *deeper* deeper) screening, only to discover that someone isn't a match. Rather than just ghosting or blocking them (unless they have done something idiotic or offensive), be clear and honest. Send something like, '*I wanted to tell you that I have enjoyed chatting with you. However, I want to be honest that there are others out there that I believe are a better match for you, and the same for me. Good luck!*'

There's no need to hurt any feelings. Just because someone is not for *you* does not mean they aren't a quality match for someone else. Consider how *you* would want to be told, delicately, that someone has decided you are not for them and use that as your guide.

The same applies to someone you haven't initiated messaging with, but who has messaged you and taken the time to read your profile. Remember the Golden Rule, '*Do unto others as you would have them do unto you.*' Something like the following will almost always be appreciated, '*Thank you so much for messaging me, but I do not think we would be a good match. Best wishes.*'

Don't act like a jerk even if you have been poorly treated before by other people. In either event, if they reply with hostility, or even excessive questions as to *why*, then it's certainly appropriate, if not advisable, to block them.

Video Chat?

Many people like to video chat (via *Skype*, *Google Hangouts*, *Face-Time*, etc.) before actually meeting. Many apps, including *Bumble* and *Tinder*, now offer it free on their platform. This can be helpful for many reasons:

1. You can verify that they are indeed the same person as seen in their profile and that the photos are current and accurate.
2. You can read their body language, listen to their voice, how they communicate, and get a sense of them without having to arrange an in-person date.
3. You may pick up on annoying habits that are a turn-off to you (like biting fingernails, never making eye contact, odd facial expressions, or whatever your pet peeves may be).

Keep in mind, though, that there are disadvantages, too. Not everyone is photogenic, and it is possible for the screen to kill an attraction that might have been there in person!

Background Check

Drumroll, please! Now that you are about to actually, possibly, *maybe,* go on a *real first date*, there's one more important screening tool you may want to use.

If you have someone's first and last name (or even just a phone number), there are background check apps and services that can be very useful. Even if you have already been able to verify someone on social media or other platforms, you can learn if they have a (relatively) clean criminal record. (Personally, I figure if someone is in their forties and has no significant felonies, they're probably safe enough for me to meet for a first date.)

You can also learn if someone has judgments against them, has filed for bankruptcy, been married more times than they have stated, still lives with their ex, and more.

Decision Fatigue

If all of this seems like a lot, you're not wrong. Screening effectively requires you to make dozens or hundreds of decisions, small and large. During my journey, I often would reach a point where I simply didn't want to look at any more profiles, swipe anymore, or ask any questions. I had also noticed that my decisions seemed to become worse. I became less focused on what I wanted or allowed poor matches to slip through my funnel. Those feelings would fade, but I came to understand that I was experiencing *decision fatigue.*

Researchers have found that we have a limited number of decisions that we can make each day without beginning to tire because decisions take great mental effort. As we fatigue, we make increasingly worse decisions over the day. Even Judges make poorer-quality decisions late in the day versus early.

Dating can make the problem worse because we are social creatures. A "like" can trigger a dopamine rush in our brain, lighting up the reward centers in the brain and increasing our motivation and arousal. As a result, we can become addicted to receiving likes and texts. With each notification, our dopamine spikes, and like an addict, we want to check our phone for our *reward*, which is a positive feeling.

Women especially want to be well-liked by men. We want to attract and please a potential partner, so much so that it can affect our self-identity, and keep us swiping, messaging, and screening far past the point that decision fatigue has set in.

An extremely large inventory of potential matches, although exciting at first, can eventually become detrimental. I fell prey to this initially, swiping left and right over hundreds of men. I engaged in conversation with guys who were completely wrong for me, wasting even more time and effort.

Politicians and top-level executives battle this same problem. To combat it, some may have only two or three basic outfit choices to limit their morning wardrobe decision-making, freeing up more energy to process truly important decisions. Eventually, I limited myself to checking app messages only during the evening, and only for fifteen minutes, *if* I still had the energy. If not, I waited until the following day or weekend. By limiting myself, I kept my filters clean, and my decisions strong.

Some dating services allow you to see who likes or right-swipes you *first*. Even though *Tinder* and *Bumble* are free, I opted to pay for the premium service for this reason. That way, I only had to weed through guys who already selected me, rather than having to swipe over dozens of guys per day, hoping they had or would right-swipe me as well.

While an abundance of choice is nice, and certainly is an ego boost, having too many choices can be overwhelming. I encountered many men who swiped me and were very enthusiastic at first. Over time, however, the contact declined. Instead of trying to engage in a meaningful conversation with me, they continued to swipe on other women, chasing the next bit of dopamine excitement.

There is nothing wrong with this *per se*. But ask yourself, does a never-ending stream of swiping get you closer to your goal? Or is it better to follow through with someone you matched, get to know them a little better through your screening, and then either move forward with the relationship or unmatch if they are not a fit? The length of the line waiting to meet you isn't nearly as important as the *quality* of the people in it.

To avoid decision fatigue, and keep a healthy relationship with dating apps, I strongly recommend limiting your online dating and messaging to pre-determined times during the day or night. You might be surprised at how quickly these apps can take over your life and affect your productivity, your energy, and even your mental health.

* * *

Congratulations—you've now reached near-professional screening skill levels! You are one step closer to finding your dream relationship. In the next chapter, we'll show you how to make the most of the exciting world of dating in person!

CHAPTER 9

The First Date

How on earth can you explain in terms of chemistry and physics so important a biological phenomenon as first love? Put your hand on a stove for a minute, and it seems like an hour. Sit with that special girl for an hour, and it seems like a minute. That's relativity.

-Albert Einstein

You made it! You've prepared, screened, and screened deeper still, and finally, you're about to schedule a date with a good potential match or already have one coming up.

This is truly a milestone. Many people launch themselves into first dates with no idea of what they want, and no idea if the person sitting in front of them is even *close* to a match. It takes time, patience, and courage to make it this far. Congratulations on your hard work!

If it feels like your journey thus far has been somewhat of a rollercoaster, you're not alone. I have met some wonderful men through my dating experiences, and I have also been deeply disappointed, grossly lied to, and royally pissed off by others. The roller coaster is very real.

I don't, however, regret any parts of the ride! Each moment, good or bad, was a learning experience that taught me about myself, men, women, and human psychology. Now, I'm that much closer to my dream relationship. I'm crystal clear about what I want, what works for me, and what doesn't. More importantly, I know how to quickly find out if a man isn't a good fit—an essential skill for not wasting time and staying out of difficult situations.

In this chapter, I'll give you the insights and recommendations you need to understand the background for the first date and sail through it with ease. Some are just good old common sense, and some will be counterintuitive. All will provide context and help you know what to look for, what to expect, and how to develop rules on how to behave.

Don't let the excitement and anticipation of a date get the better of you and lead you to continue with a bad match. And if you do find a compatible match, you want to behave in a way that attracts them to you and moves the relationship forward!

Attraction and Sex

Yep, we're going straight to sex. And for a good reason—so many people go straight there as well!

Often, when we are attracted to someone, and that feeling is reciprocated, we tend to jump into bed far too soon without thinking about the long-term. It's understandable—there's no doubt that the initial infatuation phase of dating *just feels good*. The brain produces strong chemicals like oxytocin and dopamine that flood the body and can blind us to faults, and things that we know are *not* a good fit for us in a long-term partner. But when we finally get over that feel-good phase, and the blinders come off, that's when we discover we're too deep into a bad relationship. That's when people get hurt.

This chapter isn't about hook-ups, friends with benefits, or other casual sex arrangements. If that's what both parties want and consent to, that's great. Sometimes, especially when you are trying to get over a relationship or build your confidence, or when you are not emotionally available to start a new relationship, it can even be preferable. Something casual can offer companionship and fun with another person, without getting too emotionally involved with a mismatch.

For me, one-night stands feel empty. They aren't a fit. Since I'm looking for a long-term relationship and am absolutely ready for it, I need to get to know the person first, to establish trust, and make sure that he's intelligent, kind, and someone I genuinely like. Only when I am reasonably certain that there is strong potential will I move on to a sexual relationship.

Not only do I want to be sure that the man is a good match, but I also want to make sure that he's really into *me* and *who I really am*, not just driven by physical attraction. *To do this requires observing someone's actions and behaviors over time.* It's for this reason that I bring my full authentic self to dating, both in my profile and in person. I want to make sure a guy is into *all* of me, including my imperfections. Establishing a relationship over false or physical-only pretenses doesn't last in the long term, and trust either never develops or erodes quickly once the proverbial cat's out of the bag.

Instead of putting on a fake persona, concealing your true self, or misleading or lying because you want to make another person like you, be authentic from the start. The best relationships form and last when both people can truly be themselves—open, vulnerable, and honest with each other.

First Date Specifics

The first date is important for so many reasons. First, it's often only in person that you can truly feel chemistry, or the lack thereof. Second, many behaviors and much of body language can only be seen in person. Someone may be a good match on paper and make it through your screening funnel, but that doesn't guarantee you'll be attracted to them, or that their actions (or even looks) will match their words (or photos).

How soon?

Once you have reached the point where you really like someone, they meet all of your *musts* and many of your *likes*, and there are no apparent red flags, I generally recommend meeting as soon as possible.

I prefer this to texting, talking on the phone, or video chatting for an extended period. The point is to quickly find potential chemistry and energy matches and weed out the rest. That's best done in person. If there is a fit for both of you, you'll want to progress to the next level instead of continuing to swipe on other matches forever. It's critical, then, to find out if there is a potential for further and specifically physical attraction for both sides.

Note that *most of your first dates will not lead to second dates*! This is as it should be. You are looking to *disqualify* the other person (and they should be doing the same). You are *not* trying to force it, or "make it work," but to feel if it flows naturally. If you don't feel chemistry on a first date and the person never calls you back, don't be discouraged—be grateful! Clearly, that person is *not* the person of your dream relationship. Simply move on.

Your prior steps and homework thus far will have eliminated a *lot* of awful dates and wasted time, but be prepared: *you will have bad dates.* You can't screen everyone online.

The good news is that you'll gain valuable experience on every date—good, bad, or in between. I made two good male friends and have gone into business with a third—all of whom I went on first dates with. They were solid guys and good potential matches, and although the necessary attraction wasn't there, I gained a lot.

Where to?

For your first date, I recommend meeting for coffee or drinks at a public place. This is for two reasons. First, safety should always be a priority, particularly on a first date with someone you've never met. Be sure to share the person's full name and photo with one of your friends as a backup security measure, along with where you're going, when you leave, and when you return safely. Take your own car, Uber, or Lyft. No matter how well-intended a first date seems, do not allow them to pick you up. If at any moment during the date, you feel uncomfortable, leave, and leave quickly. *Always* trust your gut.

The second reason I advocate meeting for just coffee or drinks on a first date is that if you know quickly that you have no interest, you can make a quick and clean getaway within minutes, rather than hours. That said, everyone is different. If you prefer a lengthier outing—to a restaurant you like or to hear a band you enjoy—go for it! Even if you don't like the person, you'll be doing something you enjoy. Another option I like for first dates is a walk at a public park or nature trail. This is a safe option, allows for private conversation, and you can get your body moving and boost your Vitamin D at the same time!

If you feel like you have developed a good rapport with someone already, and you are excited about meeting them in person, then a meal may be a good idea, as it gives you more time to get to know each other. Even if there's no chemistry, you'll have met an interesting person, and perhaps even a new friend.

Make sure you go to a relatively quiet and well-lit place; you want to be able to see your partner's body language, facial expressions, eye contact, and demeanor. Avoid bars where it's too loud. You'll spend all evening shouting and only hearing every other word.

Who pays?

Even in this enlightened time, my experience has been that a man usually pays for the first date—coffee, meal, or otherwise.

Your offer to pay half can sometimes be insulting for a man, but there is also something to be said for a man not feeling like you used him for a free meal! The choice is yours. If it's important to you as a woman that a man pays (again, remember, these are *your* requirements!), and you offer to pay half, his response will be insightful.

If he clearly expects you to pay half—by asking the server for two checks, for example—you will have learned this as well. These are just some of the many things that are hard to discover without actually going on a date.

How do you (and more importantly, they) behave?

When you arrive, put your phone on silent and in your pocket or purse. There is nothing more annoying than someone looking at their phone instead of you, and the same is true for your date. Even if the person is not a good fit, staring at your phone or texting your bestie is inconsiderate and won't change the situation. Think about how you would feel if he were texting or took a random phone call in the middle of a date.

You should be fully engaged, and 100% focused on the other person, as they should be on you. No calls, no texts, no daydreaming, no checking out the cute barista. If your date is not engaged, or there is simply no chemistry, you can leave and do your post-game texting elsewhere.

Your process so far should ensure that you won't end up on a date with a total fraud or POS (piece of shit). But for the person who just isn't a fit, simply say, "It really was nice to meet you. I have to go and meet up with some of my friends." It's that easy. You don't owe a first date much of your time, but being kind is simply good policy. Be polite, but be clear and move on. Other fish await!

During your date, watch for examples of the qualities or attributes the other person exhibits from your wish and do-not-wish lists. Stay in the moment and observe not just the other person, but also *yourself*. How do you feel around them? Do you feel positive? Do you feel excited? Is your body telling you that you like this person, that you are attracted to them? Do you feel butterflies? Do they lift your energy, or drag it down? Do you feel anything "off," like annoyance, boredom, or even worse, *disgust*? A strong negative reaction will *not* improve on future dates—cut your losses politely and move on.

After chemistry, be attuned to your date's behavior during the date. Do they talk only about themselves, or do they ask questions about you as well? Watch their body language carefully. How open or closed are they? How often do they smile? How do you like their voice, the way they express themselves, and their mannerisms? Do they keep looking at their phone (or worse, actually texting or talking to someone), or are they focused on you? Are they courteous to the wait staff, or are they impatient or arrogant? What types of things do they talk about or ask? Is the conversation filled with shallow or small talk, or do you discuss important things designed to get to know each other better? Does your date maintain eye contact with you? Are there off-putting sexual innuendos, messages, or advances? If you are a woman, does he walk you to your car? (For you male readers, if you act like a gentleman—open the door for your date, pull out her chair, smile at her, and truly engage—you are more likely to get a second date if you want one.)

Be unapologetically yourself during the date. Be authentic and vulnerable. It takes courage to show your full self, but it's worth it. Researcher Brené Brown's brilliant work on vulnerability teaches us that it takes courage to be fully authentic, and it's worth it to take the risk, even when you fail. Show up as the best version of yourself, despite your flaws and imperfections. Being honest and confident are two of the most attractive characteristics you can offer to a quality partner.

Remember, too, that what you consider to be flaws or imperfections may be acceptable compromises, if not *attractive* to a person who is a good match for you. They may also be a complete turn-off to someone who is not. In either case, you win by being yourself. Do you really want to spend time pretending you are someone else just to please the wrong person? Or alienating the right one? There's no value in getting people to like you for who you are *not*.

What do you talk about?

In addition to watching your date's behavior, be sure to ask qualifying and disqualifying questions from your screening questionnaire. You are, after all, trying to get to the bottom of who they are, what interests them, what values and beliefs they have, and whether there are any deal-breakers. Do not give them any clues about the answers. If you see a red line behavior, it's time to leave.

Make the most of the date. Don't waste much time on small talk about the weather and traffic. This isn't an inquisition, but you do want to get to know the person well enough to either say goodbye or consider a second date.

Learning about your date is easier than you think. People love to talk about themselves—it's the favorite topic of most human beings, other than extreme introverts, so get your date talking! Ask them about their interests, passions, likes and dislikes, and life experiences. Be genuinely curious. Asking questions is the best way to learn how they think, why they do things, and what motivates them. More importantly, it will help you decide whether you want to move forward with a second date or not. As a side bonus, it will make you a better conversationalist. That's a skill that will always serve you.

Be sure, however, that the conversation flows both ways—after all, they should be just as interested in getting to know you. Are they asking you probing questions to get to know you, or are they bragging about their high school football career, how accomplished they are in their job, or the beauty pageants they won umpteen years ago? If your date is into you, they should want to get to know who you *really* are.

Remember: the goal on a first date is to get to know this person well enough to either disqualify them or to continue to a second date. As such, you should expect far more first dates than seconds. Most first dates won't go anywhere because of a lack of chemistry or fit but don't take it personally. Each person you disqualify is helping you get closer to the right match!

Second date?

More often than not, you'll know after the first date if someone is *not* for you. They will also usually know if you aren't for them. Generally, a mismatch is much easier to spot than a potential match, which can and should take more time.

No!

Don't try to use a second date to turn a bad match into a good one. If you aren't attracted to the other person at all, then a *no* is a *no*. A deal-breaker is a deal-breaker. No second date needed. More time will *not* change the person in front of you. The same applies to later dates. Whether it's after the first date or the twentieth, if you're not interested in someone, let them know. It's better to (potentially) hurt their feelings now than later. Dragging things out helps neither of you.

As difficult as it may be, being able to deal with emotions, even negative ones, is a necessary skill for successful dating. Be a decent human being, and never, *ever* ghost. When a second date is a *no*, but the other person still appears to be interested, take responsibility, and end it courteously and respectfully. You can also offer friendship if that's an option.

Do *not* rationalize a second date with someone because they are wealthy or successful. Women, in particular, tend to be attracted to these qualities—learn to look past them. I refused a second date with a guy who was extremely wealthy because I wasn't attracted to him, and there was no chance I would ever be. Money will not buy happiness or contentment in a relationship, period.

Not only should you not rationalize a second date, but be aware that you can't *force* one either. If the other person is not interested, they're not interested. It doesn't matter how much *you* are.

Often, this will be quite obvious. If they do not express any intention of follow-up contact or are direct enough to tell you (hopefully nicely) that you aren't a match, then it's time to move on. Someone may seem enthusiastic towards you on a first date but then vanish. This has happened to me on more than one occasion, and will no doubt happen to you as well.

Women, if a guy does not communicate with you right away after a date—if he is not actively *pursuing* you—then accept that, for whatever reason, he's not into you, and quickly move on. Men, if you don't hear from a woman after a date, keep in mind that many women, even in the 21st century, still wait for a man to call or text first. If you do reach out and she does not reply, the same rules apply: she's not into you. Go back to your search.

If you do discover that the other person is not interested, *do not try to find out why.* This will be oh-so-tempting when you think the date went fine, or when you believe there was a connection. But most of the time, for both men and women, there will be no explanation other than a lack of chemistry (and this is particularly true if you've done your screening ahead of time). Resist the temptation to dig deeper. Do you really want to force someone to hurt your feelings or make you feel less than you are? You may have simply looked different in person than expected. There may be things he loved about you, but some things he didn't. Maybe he was having a terrible day, and it had nothing to do with you! It doesn't matter what the reason is, looking for it will not help you. Move on.

Yes!

If you both are certain you want a second date, then the answer to this question is easy: *yes.* Definitely go on a second date. If you liked the person well enough, if you have chemistry, if they meet your initial screening criteria, and assuming they want to see you again, you absolutely should move on to a second date. Yes!

Maybe ...

I have learned that, at least for me, if there is no chemistry during the first date, there is probably never going to be. That means there is probably no need for a second date—I will only be wasting time and money.

I do, however, know many people who have gone on second dates with partners they felt they had a good connection with on the first date but didn't necessarily feel *chemistry* with. Over time, they did end up developing chemistry—it was just slow to spark.

If you like the other person, they meet your screening criteria, but you're unsure about chemistry, I would consider a second date. It can take time for some people to build real attraction. Generally, men know they are attracted to a woman quickly (some can tell based on photos alone), and for women, it takes more time.

Keep in mind, too, that even if a second or third date does not result in a romantic connection, you may make a friend. I once met a globe-traveling management consultant, and we clicked mentally and socially. There was no attraction, however, at least not on my part, and I knew there was no potential. At the end of the date, he asked me for a second date. I said I would be happy to meet him again as a friend. To my surprise, he said, "Karen, I would *love* to be your friend!" And so it was. (And don't forget—quality people often have quality friends. You never know where a connection might take you.)

Delay "engagement"

I'm talking specifically about emotional engagement, not a *ring*, but this principle applies to both! For the love of God, please do not get emotionally engaged after a first date, no matter how well you think it may have gone. Try to resist even during the second or third dates if you can.

Even if your date wants to see you again and you feel confident about mutual chemistry, try to avoid becoming emotionally engaged until you reach something more than a pleasant first date, nice words, or even a kiss. Withhold your full engagement until you have genuinely connected with your partner on a deeper level— even if it takes ten dates!

I've learned not to engage emotionally, even when early signs are good until my match's actions and behavior confirm my feelings. This means they text me right after a date, and the next day (and the next...), immediately ask me out again and follow through. Their interest is obvious because they are actively *pursuing* me—I can tell by their *actions*. Always, *always* choose to believe actions over words.

Do not play games

Just as there are no rules for dating, there should be no games either. If a man waits a day or a few days after a date to contact a woman in order not to seem too eager or needy, he's sending the wrong message. A woman who waits before responding to a man to play hard to get is likewise playing games and confusing everyone. Be genuine in your behavior.

If you are eager, passionate, and excited about your date, don't wait to show it, even if you risk rejection. By the same token, if you are not interested in seeing your date again, honestly communicate that when asked for a second date.

Men, if you do ask a woman for a second date, make sure you mean it and follow through. If you are not interested in her, do not ask her out again just to keep your options open or to give your ego a boost. You are unnecessarily hurting the woman's feelings if you ask her out and then never text or call.

Instead, be courteous, thank her for the time you spent together, and leave it at that. (Ladies, understand that if he does *not* mention another date, or follow up with you, then he does not *want* another date with you. The reason doesn't matter—*leave it alone!*) Gentlemen, if a woman (who doesn't heed this advice) follows up with you for a second date, it's time to politely explain that you did not feel chemistry or that she is not your type or whatever you feel is appropriate in the situation. This avoids drama and bad feelings for all concerned.

First dates in a nutshell? Mutual, authentic attraction and interest is the only reason to move forward. Otherwise, keep swiping!

CHAPTER 10

Real First Date Stories

A life's worth, the end isn't measured in hours, or dollars. It's measured by the amount of love exchanged along the way.

-Douglas Means

It's one thing to understand the background for the first date and to have some rules in mind for how to behave and what to look for. But there's nothing like real dates to help you learn. As you prepare for yours, I'm going to share some real stories from my first dates (good and bad!), including descriptions of the men and their profiles. I'll share stories of my dates, including, inevitably, some of the *bad* ones.

Before we start, let me offer a disclaimer: I do not want to stereotype or demonize men. But since I only date men, it is only men with whom I have had such bad (as well as *great*) experiences. A heterosexual man writing a similar book would have similar horror stories about women. Naturally, you'll only be seeing things from my perspective, since you are looking through my lens as my first-hand experiences, but every story has a lesson to offer.

My dad used to ask me a question: *What is the difference between a smart person and a stupid person?* The answer is that a stupid person learns only from their own mistakes, whereas a smart person can learn from the mistakes of others. While my experiences are specific to me, the lessons I learned are universal. Fortunately, you get to be the smart person who learns from my mistakes!

GQ Jeff

Jeff was gorgeous – "super-hot" was how I first described him. He was so good-looking that at first I was convinced he wasn't real and had stolen his photos from *GQ Magazine.*

Jeff was divorced and had no children, and apparently, he had an engineering degree. Despite my concerns, I was intrigued and decided to see what he was like.

I texted him through the app first, trying to figure out if he was actually looking for a long-term relationship or whether he was a player (my intuition was telling me it was the latter). I quickly learned that he was intelligent, loved to travel internationally, and really liked and wanted children (his ex couldn't have them). He said he was okay with my daughter's young age. All his answers were right on, and apparently, mine were as well, so we planned a lunch date.

During the date, Jeff was charming and open, and I felt like he was attracted to me. The date flowed well, and he was entertaining and attentive. He took opportunities to touch my hands while asking questions about my new Fitbit, he took my hand into his and gently touched it while he was "checking it out." I could tell in person that he was physically fit, but I also learned from our conversation that he was into healthy eating as well, a big plus for me.

While Jeff was talking about his life, his adventures, and the admittedly exciting things he still wanted to do, I began to sense that his bachelor lifestyle seemed to be pretty well-established. I wondered if, at age 48, it might be difficult for him to adjust to a committed lifestyle, much less one involving a small child. I began to ask questions to assess his willingness to adapt his life to a situation like mine.

It didn't take long to discover that Jeff wasn't looking for a relationship with a woman with a small child, or someone who would be "tied down" to any significant degree by family. We parted ways.

Now, if I had been looking for a fling, I definitely would have gone further with him. (He was drop-dead gorgeous ... *duh*!) But because I was looking for a serious relationship, there was no point in going down that road, no matter how much fun it might have been.

Security Sam

In one of my best first dates, I met a man who was burned out after two years of go-nowhere dating. Sam was a security expert and skilled in detecting lies. He seemed enamored with me, telling me I was the only date he'd had who was authentic and truthful. Then he asked me, point-blank, *"You are so incredible, seemingly too good to be true. What are your faults?"*

This question isn't typically first date material, but I decided to answer his question honestly. I told him my two most significant issues were that I was almost obsessive about cleanliness and that I was still working through my emotional eating issues.

None of that seemed to scare him off. If anything, it seemed to attract him more. He immediately took my hand, gave me a hug and kiss, and thanked me for sharing with him.

Sam wasn't a long-term fit for me, but I learned that being honest and vulnerable is appreciated. Even revealing information that might be considered unappealing won't automatically scare someone off. And if it does, it simply means that you aren't a good match. Being very authentic, even on a first date, can pay off.

Awesome Amit

I matched with a handsome Indian man on Bumble who used his real first name. After the initial niceties, our text conversation went like this:

Karen: *So, Amit, why have you never married? And no kids?*

Amit: *I have been engaged, but the marriage and kids just haven't happened for numerous reasons, but I would say timing more than anything. It hasn't been a matter of want.*

Karen: *When did your last serious relationship end?*

Amit: *Earlier this year... and you?*

Karen: *Over 3 years ago, my ex moved out. Officially divorced over a year.*

Amit: *How many kids do you have? Ages? Are you originally from GA?*

Karen: *One girl, 8 years old. I was born outside of the USA. You?*

Amit: *I was born in India... moved to the USA as a child. Do you feel comfortable texting? It may be easier than on this.*

Karen: *Sure, what's your name and number?*

When he sent his name and number, I looked him up, and he was friends on Facebook with my coworker Raju, who knew him because he was friends with her husband. Raju's confirmation made him the quickest background check ever, and I had no hesitation sending him my full name and information.

Karen: *I have to admit I "looked you up" (had to make sure you're not a serial killer!) and figured out you know Raju! It's such a small world, Amit. Very small, apparently especially for Indian professionals in Atlanta. So funny!*

Amit: *I totally get it and don't blame you. Women have it a lot worse than guys … smart of you.*

Karen: *Want to switch to a call?*

Amit: *Sure, but I must warn you that my voice is very sexy, so you will have to try and focus.*

Karen: *I will do my best not to fall off the couch. :)*

We ended up having a very pleasant phone conversation and quickly decided to plan our first date. We had a great conversation in person at a romantic restaurant and hit it off on many levels. But while Amit was a great guy, he wasn't a fit for me. There was no particular reason, just not enough of the invisible, mysterious chemistry and compatibility.

Doctor Doug

Doug is a successful doctor from Denver who I matched with while on a Colorado ski trip. We connected right before I left, so we were unable to meet on the trip, but we continued to text and talk on the phone over the next few days.

It became apparent to me that Doug was a genuinely nice person and someone I would like to meet. We shared similar interests, and our conversations flew smoothly.

When I told Doug I had a few free days the week of New Year's because my daughter was going to be with her dad, he invited me to come to Las Vegas. There was no discussion of who would pay or where I would stay—not even innuendo that I would stay with him, a man I had never met. Doug simply booked a plane ticket and a hotel room for me in Vegas in a separate hotel.

He was an absolute gentleman and did not try to take advantage of the situation by imposing himself. Instead, we went out, had a great time, and got to know each other with no expectations. It was very nice and much appreciated. We didn't have chemistry, it turned out, but developed a friendship and have remained friends to this day.

Rogue Rob

I had a unique first date that took over *six months* to happen. Rob was from Australia and had an extraordinary profile. He looked sweet, fun, and unusual, and had a daughter close to the same age as mine. I came across him when I was on a ski vacation with my daughter. He was skiing in Vail at the same time. After some cursory small-talk texting on the app, we had the following conversation.

Rob: *What brings such a gorgeous lady to this app?*

Karen: *Looking to meet extraordinary people and make friend-ships, and maybe beyond if sparks fly...*

Rob: *I see. Have you had any on here yet? Come to Australia, and I guarantee sparks.*

Karen: *Met a few great people so far. One spark, but he's not ready. We stayed friends, though.*

Rob: *Well then ... what's your favorite food? Drink?*

Karen: *Anything chocolate! Favorite drink is Baileys. U?*

Rob: *Yummm. Love Japanese, Vietnamese, Spanish, and Italian food. Love red wine, champagne, Vodka. Food is pretty good here in*

Vail. You can be my guide in Atlanta.

Karen: *Yes, it is, and sure. Happy to be a food critic/guide.*

Rob: *I will do the same in Sydney. Or in Asia.*

Karen: *Don't challenge me, or I'll have to do it!*

Rob: *Bring it on! BTW, how tall are you?*

Karen: *5'9" without heels. 175cm for you. So you don't have to Google it. LOL*

Rob: *Haha, you are hilarious. We are a very similar height. Deal-breaker?*

Karen: *No, your height is not a deal-breaker. But one lie, and we're done, even as friends. Say what you mean and mean what you say.*

Rob: *Hehe cool, good to know.*

Karen: *A beard might be a deal-breaker, though. LOL.*

Rob: *What!!! Let's call it quits then!! No one complained about my beard, not even during kissing!*

Karen: *Well, you asked! Good night. Maybe we can chat tomorrow.*

Rob: *Awww ... night gorgeous Karen.*

...

Rob: *Hey! Did you miss me today?*

Karen: *Hey to you! I skied from 9-4:15. Took the last chair up.*

Rob: *Wow ... you're a pro!*

Karen: *When I ski, I must say, I go all out.*

Rob: *Well, I am impressed and keen to find out more over a dinner date.*

Karen: *Definitely, but not tomorrow. It is supposed to snow! When it snows, they can close off the highway. It is good for skiing, though!*

Rob: *We may have to wait until Atlanta. I will be there in June. Unless you wanna meet me in NY in January.*

Karen: *Maybe we could go out for dinner with the kids while we both are still here.*

Rob: *Hmmm, probably without kids, prefartable first date! Let's target NY?*

Karen: *LOL ... I didn't know "prefartable" is a word, but I would like to claim it as mine.*

Rob: *Haha, where is damn autocorrect when you need it? PREF-ERABLE, lol.*

Karen: *Are you crazy? Have you ever been to NY in January? It's COLD!*

Rob: *Yep! I spent the whole month of January last year in Pennsylvania. It WAS effin' cold.*

Karen: *Well, BTW, I like prefartable better.*

Rob: *Haha, cheeky. What's the weather like in Atlanta?*

Karen: *In the summer, HELL hot. But in January, east coast but mild. It rarely snows.*

Rob: *It doesn't get too cold?*

Karen: *What is "too" cold? Under 20 Celsius in Australia?*

Rob: *Yep!!!*

Karen: *And BTW, do you prefer that I call you Rob or something else?*

Rob: *Haha, whichever you like. And what would you like to be called? Karen? Babe? Sexy? Sweetheart?*

Karen: *C'mon, can you answer the damn question? And Karen is fine.*

Rob: *Rob is fine too, then.*

Karen: *But if we spark, you can call me whatever you like!*

Rob: *Well, I wouldn't be talking to you if I had not felt a spark already.*

Karen: *Pictures are one thing, but no substitute to in person.*

Rob: *True!*

Karen: *In person, you either spark or not, for a potential romantic* partner. *Don't you agree?*

Rob: *Haha, I know we will spark - have a good feeling about you.*

Karen: *I have a good feeling about you too. That's why you have my number. LOL*

Rob: *Sweet dreams, gorgeous Karen. Talk tomorrow.*

Rob made it clear he wanted to meet in person. We had "clicked," at least via messaging. The next day, we messaged again about the possibility of dinner, but he said his daughter was not feeling well.

Then he abruptly disappeared. My gut feeling was that he was in Vail with another woman, or ended up hooking up with someone else he had met. Before I left, I got the following message:

Rob: *Sorry we didn't get to meet up. I hope we can meet one day?*

Karen: *Maybe when you come to Atlanta in June.*

Rob: *Is that a no to New York in January?*

Karen: *I live in Atlanta, not NY. I hope this isn't too direct, but before investing time and money on a trip to New York in Jan, there needs to be a potential for something for both of us. We don't know each other well enough yet, and whether we would spark or not.*

Rob: *Well, I would love to get to know you and see where it leads.*

Rob lived across the Pacific; he certainly wasn't an ideal fit. Yet I couldn't help but be curious. He had a very public profile and was a successful entrepreneur in Australia. He was clearly smart and successful—fulfilling both requirements for me.

The problem was, I was suspicious he was a player.

Rob was giving me the impression that he thought I was at his beck and call—that I was supposed to fly from Atlanta to New York on a whim to meet him at my expense. Yet, he wouldn't even meet me briefly in Vail for a drink to see if there was chemistry.

He also didn't make it a priority to talk by phone, only texts, which was a red flag that he wasn't serious. Most of all, he was always telling me about himself, his travels to various spots in the world, his life experiences, and opinions, but seemed to have little interest in knowing who I was and what made me tick.

Rob texted again about six months later before coming to Atlanta. Since it was local, I agreed to meet him. Admittedly, I was still interested in him. However, I didn't hear from him until the day he wanted to meet for dinner. By then, I already had plans, and since he hadn't given me any notice, I wasn't willing to change them. But when he pressed about the next night, I agreed.

When I arrived at the restaurant (which he had asked me to select), Rob was half drunk. He was attractive and very chipper, but this was a big turnoff. We hugged hello, and he pulled me close to him and did not want to let go. After that, we sat at the restaurant bar and chatted for a while. He bought me a Baileys and ordered another drink for himself. And then another.

Rob wanted to go to a nightclub, so I asked him what kind of music he liked. "House," he said, and I named one of the trendiest night clubs in Atlanta.

I am not a huge fan of nightclubs, and would rather have continued to talk and get to know him more at the restaurant. Rob never even asked what I liked or wanted—instead, we headed to the club, which was packed with a Saturday night crowd.

Rob asked for a VIP booth and ordered a bottle of Cristal champagne and a huge bottle of Gray Goose Vodka. The booth and the liquor probably cost him over $2,000—a lot of money to try to impress a first date.

I took a glass of champagne and drank a few sips, while Rob continued to drink. He urged me to drink Vodka with him, but I politely refused as I don't like it. As he got drunker, he began pouring drinks for nearby dancers. He moved in closer to me, hugged me, and then kissed me.

I kissed him back, but I wasn't feeling it. There was zero chemistry. No surprise, there—Rob was not into *me*. He just wanted to have a good time at the club, get drunk, and have sex. That may have been okay for him, but was definitely not what I was looking for.

Rob's life outside work, it turned out, was all about drinking and clubbing. That was his idea of fun, as it is for many people. It just wasn't *my* idea of fun. It never has been, not even in my twenties. I love international travel and exploring new places, cultures, and food. Experiencing each new spot in depth is so much more enriching and rewarding for me than partying. Rob and I just didn't match.

The lesson? My intuition was right yet again. Rob was looking for a party girl.

He was also persistent. He texted me the next day:

Rob: *Hello gorgeous, let's do lunch?*

Karen: *I am in the middle of my workout, so I cannot meet for lunch.*

Rob: *Then how about drinks after your workout? I thought you were drop-dead gorgeous and wanted to know more about you.*

Karen: *Maybe you have the wrong impression of me. I am not looking for one-night stands or hookups. Not me. Never was. Thanks again for the drinks last night. I hope you continue to have a blast in Hotlanta!*

I still wish Rob well and hope he finds what he's looking for. I know I will, but it won't be in a nightclub, not even at a VIP booth, complete with Cristal.

Doggie Daniel

Even with great intuition, you may not know after the first date whether someone is just looking for a fling. Daniel was a tall and attractive former athlete with a second career in sales, and described himself on his profile as, "Successful, no games, no drama, no BS, honest and loyal, great guy."

I found it odd on our first date when he talked openly about sex with his ex-girlfriends, yet also talked about how he was ready for a long-term commitment with the right woman, including marriage and children. He had never been married and did not have kids.

Still, I was attracted to Daniel, and he was saying many of the right things; when he asked me to go out again, I agreed. On our second date, he was attentive, and we had a mostly intelligent and pleasant conversation. But again, he found a way to work his sex life into the dialogue, this time going a little further, hinting at his sexual prowess. While I will never dispute that a satisfying sex life is important in a romantic relationship, a *quality* relationship requires much more than that. And a fling was not my thing.

Later, Daniel walked me to my car. I got in and put the window down, and he leaned in and kissed me. I cannot lie—it was nice; he was a good kisser. We said our goodbyes and agreed to talk the next day. But I hadn't even made it home before he texted me:

Daniel: *I want u bad.*

… <Karen hesitating> …

Karen: *I enjoyed the evening, and maybe we can get together again soon.*

Daniel: *How about now? If your daughter is home, you can come over to my place. I want u BAD.*

Karen: *What??? I am not willing to jump into bed until I'm actually sure you are the right guy for me.*

Daniel: *I am. Let's get it on tonight. I like doggie style the best. U?*

Karen: *Are you effing kidding me?? If you don't learn to respect women, you will never have a fulfilling long-term relationship if that is what you really even want. But if so, you should be aware that quality women respond better to honesty, not manipulation. I hope you can do some work on yourself and get better. I will block you now.*

And I did.

The Ghost of Alex

I once matched with a guy named Alex, who passed the initial screening, who I really liked, and who seemed to really like me. When we met in person, he was very open in discussing what he wanted in a woman, and told me, without being asked, why I appealed to him. (And no, I did not get the impression that he was just trying to get in my pants!)

We chatted some more as Alex walked me to my car, and he told me that since he was new to Atlanta, he really wanted to build a social circle with like-minded people.

I assumed that I would be hearing from him again, and I kindly offered to introduce him to some of my colleagues and friends, and even to include him in an upcoming city-wide event where many of them would be. He seemed quite interested to see me again and attend the event.

And then … nothing. I never heard from Alex again. After a few days, I violated my own rules—I was still in the learning phase at this point—and sent him a text to ask how he was doing. He didn't respond. Alex became a ghost.

I believe in closure. Even when dealing with people like "Rogue

Rob" and "Doggie Daniel" who were clearly not for me, I never ghosted them. Ghosting leaves unresolved business in our minds and can be difficult to deal with. Don't do it.

Genuine Joe

Even when there's no chemistry and romantic relationship potential, all is definitely not lost! I am sapiosexual, meaning I am sparked by intelligent and bright people, and my date with Joe was a perfect example of how connecting on a mental level could lead to an important friendship.

Karen: *So how much time do you spend in Atlanta?*

Joe: *I've been in Nashville for like a month. I'll be here for a couple of weeks, probably through the holiday, and then head back. It's usually 100% up to me. That said, I'm a Nashville resident, and the more time I spend there, the more I like it. I don't like to mislead you.*

Karen: *It's okay. We can potentially at least be friends if we like each other!*

Joe: *That sounds awesome! Like your style. You have any plans this weekend? My friends are away, so it's just the dog and me. Love the dog, but he's not much for conversation.*

Karen: *What, you can't understand his barking?*

Joe: *Haha... not really! You're divorced, right? Husband isn't going to burst into the restaurant, is he?*

Karen: *LOL. Absolutely divorced, yes.*

Joe: *Good to know! I will take your word for it.*

Karen: *You should! I can laugh about it now. Glad to share!*

Joe: *Perfect! Even more fun!*

Karen: *Just need to verify you're not a psycho first. You don't look like one, but psychos rarely do, right?*

Joe: *Eccentric, yes. Psycho, no. You need to do your Google stalking, that's why I gave my last name. Which, ahem... I don't have yours...*

Karen: *Need to verify first. I haven't had time to do a background check, yet. Don't worry. I won't ask for your SSN... YET!*

Joe: *Do you know what I do yet? Have you been Googling?*

Karen: *At the moment, I'm texting while running, so not yet.*

Joe: *No typos?! Impressive!*

Karen: *Elliptical. Saves my knees.*

Joe: *Still...*

Karen: *Wait until we meet to be impressed! LOL.*

Joe: *I'm ALREADY impressed. You appear to be a smart, sharp, confident woman who requires thoughtful humor and isn't afraid of a challenge. Well, at least that's what I've gathered so far.*

Karen: *Wow, that was very observant of you! Now I am the one impressed! LOL.*

Joe: *Oh, and can probably kick my ass...*

Karen: *Perhaps! :)*

Joe: *Major? Grad school?*

Karen: *Will tell you later. Yes, grad school. But got a much better education running my own business.*

Joe: *Assumed that. Major might disclose your job, so that's off-limits for now, right? So you have had a direction and been focused on your career for decades?*

Karen: *Yes, actually starting a new business in a totally different niche – food. Not a restaurant or anything. Something that has never been done before.*

Joe: *So I take it that mission matters as well as money. You have a soul. And you look for gaps and flaws in the status quo.*

Karen: *Absolutely. Not motivated by money. I value the journey more, although money is somewhat important for lifestyle purposes.*

Like if I want to go ski Vail, I want to do it without worrying about the cost.

Joe: *Believe you can make a difference. Ambition. Very high fear threshold. And you're proud of yourself. Am I right?*

Karen: *Yes, yes, yes, and yes.*

Joe: *So experiences over stuff? Reads business books and biographies?*

Karen: *Business books, yes. Not biographies much. Lots of psychology books.*

Joe: *So you like "winning" and being right?*

Karen: *I like a win-win. Not winning at all costs. Same about being right. I can be proven wrong. And will accept it.*

Joe: *Okay, I think I have you completely pegged now. Nobody should have you pegged.*

Karen: *Well, Joe, nobody has so far.*

Joe: *You find that annoying, don't you?*

Karen: *Actually, no!*

Joe: *Well, you're already fascinating! We share a lot of traits. Similar thought processes, too, I think. Similar influences, goals... different though. Very excited to meet you, hopefully.*

I found the conversation to be very pleasant and engaging. Joe had volunteered his full name, which enabled me to check him out, and I figured it would be safe enough to meet in person. Even though he lived in Nashville and a romantic connection was out, I thought we might pursue a friendship.

I had a lovely time. We clicked intellectually, and Joe was fascinating. He was my only date by then who seemed to have pegged me just by asking probing questions by text and analyzing my answers with his brilliant and intuitive mind. Even though Joe and I were not a match romantically, our connection was most certainly not wasted time.

To his tremendous credit, Joe is the one who pushed me to write this book and inspired me to keep looking for my match. He gave me a *huge* boost of confidence when we met in person, for which I will always be grateful. Here's an excerpt from the texts after our date:

Joe: *I think you should consider writing a book.*

Karen: *About?*

Joe: *All this dating stuff.*

Karen: *Dating stuff?*

Joe: *Human relations, perspectives, priorities, values, energy, time, family, success...*

Karen: *Other than you, who would buy it? LOL.*

Joe: *You have a pretty cool story, and you have a mind like a drill. It's engaging. Not to mention you'd look pretty good on the back cover. See what I did there? Snuck in a gratuitous compliment. Bold stuff.*

Karen: *Actually, I think a book about dating for busy people really might sell. And yes, very bold, I'm impressed.*

Joe: *Oh, I wouldn't buy it... :)*

Karen: *Yes, I suppose I would have to give you a free copy since you inspired it.*

Joe: *C'mon, it's uplifting stuff. Your perspective is valuable, and you no doubt would express it in a very appealing and relatable way.*

Karen: *What do you mean, exactly?*

Joe: *You have had a lot of choices to make, and appear to have chosen the less comfortable path a lot. But it definitely seems to be working, and you are obviously thriving and making great choices in your matches, BTW) :) That's the book!*

Karen: *Well, I do seem to have figured out generally how to weed out catfishers, sleazes, and assholes, and generally only go out with* real *people and those I am attracted to.*

Joe: *So you could tell instantly that I was real? And that you're oddly attracted to me? :)*

Karen: *I'm definitely attracted to your brain. Isn't that the most romantic thing you ever heard?*

Joe: *Um ... perhaps 2nd most...*

Karen: *Okay, well almost had it.*

Joe: *I like your brain too ... it's magical.*

Karen: *Why, thank you, Joe. And that's why I hope we can actually be friends, TRUE friends.*

Joe: *Yes, Karen, I am very excited to know you. And would be honored to be your friend.*

Karen: *That is so good to hear, Joe. And you are proof that good things do come out of these sites!*

I sincerely appreciated meeting Joe, and ultimately, we developed a genuine friendship. He has an extraordinary mind, and this book would not exist without him. I will be eternally grateful for his inspiration and friendship.

Handsome Hemant

When a first date clicks, it just clicks. Your intuition and your body know it, and you react positively.

Hemant was different, in a good way. He was from India, had traveled the world, and previously lived in both New York and Los Angeles. His unique profile characteristics had a massive appeal to me. He claimed to be empathetic and intelligent, and he had a kind, gorgeous smile that lit up his face. After reading his profile thoroughly, I swiped right and initiated the conversation:

Karen: *Hey, Hemant. I'm Karen, and your profile is great. What kind of work do you do?*

Hemant: *Honestly, I have never had anyone ask me this as the first question. Don't you want to know if I am an addict, cheater, fake, or all of the above? LOL*

Karen: *I'm sure that if you were an addict, cheater, fake, or douche-bag, you would not actually admit it. But don't think I won't find out! LOL. Whether you are is not a question for an online chat, but something to observe in action, including responses to my questions. So you'd better watch out!*

Hemant: *Ha! "Douchebags" … sorry I left that one out. I call them shmucks. LOL If I may ask, you definitely don't sound southern, or, no offense, southern "ladies" don't usually throw out "douchebag!"*

Karen: *Definitely not southern. During my limited online dating experience, I have encountered some douchebags, that's for sure. I am just cautious until I meet the person and can decide for myself. But I've had good dates with solid guys too.*

Hemant: *I can understand being cautious, especially for a woman. With me being an introvertish extrovert, online works for me. I have had my share of craziness too!*

We continued to chat a bit, and then he sent me his name and Facebook and Instagram names.

Hemant: *So now that you have my 411, hopefully, you know I am real. :)*

Karen: *Many thanks for giving out your name so quickly. From my experience, the legit guys do that.*

Hemant: *Well, I am excited to connect with you, Karen.*

After I checked Hemant out online, we spoke on the phone. He seemed intelligent and unique, and we quickly made a dinner date. I figured that if I could spend thirty minutes with him on the phone and not be bored or turned off, I certainly wouldn't be bored at dinner.

After our phone conversation, Hemant texted me a quote:

Silence is essential. We need silence, just as much as we need air, just as much as plants need light. If our minds are crowded with words and thoughts, there is no space for us.

And then he added:

I really enjoyed talking with you. Love your energy! So looking forward to seeing you tomorrow. Goodnight! XO

My instincts were right. Hemant was charming and intriguing in person, and the evening flew by. He asked me to text him when I got home, which I did, and we planned to meet again the next day.

Hemant then freed up his entire weekend after our Friday date, to be able to spend more quality time together. Our date on Saturday lasted six hours and was magical.

Hemant and I ended up having a 10-month loving relationship, and even though we broke up, we are great friends to this day.

* * *

A great first date is a stepping stone—one point in the process of getting to know someone to gauge your attraction and compatibility, and ultimately decide whether to go further.

That decision, however, isn't always easy. In the next chapters, I'll offer tools and tips to help evaluate your partner for long-term compatibility and grow a new match into your dream relationship!

CHAPTER 11

Next-Level Dating

Love recognizes no barriers. It jumps hurdles, leaps fences, penetrates walls to arrive at its destination full of hope.

-Maya Angelou

If you haven't skipped ahead, then you have by now had your first date, or perhaps even a handful of them! And if one of those dates is headed towards a second, or even third or fourth, it means you've had easy-flowing conversations, you really liked the person, and you are reasonably sure they feel the same way about you.

If those things are all true, then your body is definitely producing those feel-good chemicals that are so exciting when you see your date's name pop up on your phone, never mind when you hug or kiss them.

"The One"

With those chemicals flooding your system, it'll be tempting to believe you've found "the one" – that singular, perfect person who is your "one and only," and your true "soul mate."

You haven't.

If you believe that there is just one person for you and your goal is to find him or her out of the almost eight billion people on this earth, you're setting yourself up for failure. Don't believe the *Hollywood* fantasies and fairytales that are so deeply rooted in us.

This should be good news, however, not bad. It means there are *multiple* potential partners you can ultimately create a quality long-term relationship with. If there is more than one person out there for you, just think about how that increases your odds of finding your dream relationship!

Whether you meet one of these many possible partners and hit it off is a combination of *luck* (time, place, availability, etc.) which is outside your control, and your *actions and attitude*—things like preparation, good intentions, authenticity, and being proactive, all of which are *within* your control. Your job is to choose to control what you can and be prepared for when luck meets opportunity. That's a rule that has served me well in both my business *and* personal lives.

Subsequent Dates

After a date or two with the same person, consider changing things up a little. Go on a nature walk, to a comedy show, another fun activity, or out with friends (yours or theirs). Avoid the temptation to go to the same restaurant or do the same thing as last time.

Mixing things up gives you a chance to observe your partner in different environments and social settings. The kinds of friends and acquaintances they have will tell you even more. Do they behave consistently across the board? Are the two of you having increasingly deeper conversations that are easy and natural, or do they feel difficult or forced? Do they communicate effectively with you? Are they open to your ideas and suggestions?

These subsequent dates are also an excellent opportunity to ask about prior relationships. You'll also learn more details about children and relationships with parents and other family members. Freud may be long dead, but some of his theories still hold today.

You'll also want to delve deeper into what type of relationship they are seeking. Don't just take their word for what they wrote on their profile. This is the time to start actively looking for red flags and deal-breakers. Ideally, your pre-date screening and funnel will have weeded out most deal-breakers before you ever go on a date. But *people lie*—sometimes without knowing it themselves. These subsequent dates are a chance to get a deeper and more reliable sense of whether both of you are ready to move forward. Does his idea of a long-term relationship mean a weekend and traveling companion only, and you want him to move in with you? Does he want a partner less successful, and you want an equal? Is she not as affectionate as you like?

After a few dates, a weekend or short trip away is always a good idea. It's helpful to see people out of their element and in a new environment with you. I would recommend waiting until after you've spent a few weekends together in your hometown. You need to be sure you are completely safe, and that you are comfortable sexually with your partner. (More about S-E-X coming soon!) You also need to have some comfort level that the two of you are moving forward in your relationship; the silent three-hour drive back home on a Sunday morning after one of you breaks it off on Saturday night will be awkward at best.

As your relationship grows, be sure to continue to enjoy your life much as it was before. Continue with the activities you enjoy, and spend time with your friends as usual. It's not healthy to neglect your friends while focusing all your time and energy on a partner, and if it doesn't work out with your partner, your friends will still be there. Plus, if you become fixated on the other person, you risk scaring them off (more on this in the "For Ladies Only" chapter). In any case, continuing your normal activities can help to feel out your new potential partner, revealing any control issues or obsessive tendencies as well as taking it slow.

There is nothing wrong with including your new significant other in your circle of friends and hobbies in moderation. And participating in a hobby together certainly can enhance the relationship. You can either try one of theirs, or vice versa, combine both hobbies or try something new to both of you. Many people love their hobbies; being receptive to that part of your partner and enjoying their passion with them is not only insightful but fun!

You can also use subsequent dates to watch for boundaries—both theirs and yours. If you have made your boundaries clear and they are violated, simply walk away. If you don't think the boundary was violated intentionally, you can offer a person a second chance, especially early on.

Don't expect people to know what your boundaries are unless you tell them; none of us are mind readers. For example, I have a personal boundary about not arguing with a partner in front of my daughter. In my opinion, there's a time and place for that, that doesn't include a child being present. If my partner doesn't know about this boundary, I can explain that to him. But if he violates it a second time, I would consider ending the relationship. Most unacceptable behavior does not improve with time!

Respect yourself. Do not bend your boundaries just to please another person. They will only continue to push other boundaries, walk over you, and will eventually lose respect for you. Worse, you will lose yourself in the process as well. Boundaries are as important for your self-esteem as they are for a relationship. In any relationship, romantic or otherwise, you need to maintain your independence—without boundaries, your partner will not be able to respect you.

If, however, you genuinely believe that changing your behavior for a partner will benefit *you*, then do it. I have a friend who bites her fingernails, and it drove her boyfriend crazy. There was nothing wrong with him asking her to try to stop. The habit was annoying, and stopping wasn't an unreasonable request, but more than that, the change was going to benefit *her*. Do you have any quirky or annoying behaviors that bother your partner? (Well, of *course*, you do!)

I prefer clean-shaven guys because I have sensitive skin. When I kiss my man passionately, stubble hurts my face. If I request that he shave more often, with this explanation, and the guy doesn't bother to do so, I can assume that he doesn't care enough about me to change something relatively small.

Kissing, Foreplay, and Beyond

Presumably, almost everyone kisses their date or potential partner first before moving straight to sex (although that all may be rolled up into the same evening!).

But even before kissing—whether you are the man or the woman initiating it—make sure the other person is comfortable with a close physical touch from you.

For a first kiss, even when emotions are high, I recommend asking for permission or telling them in advance—something like, "I am so intrigued by you, and I am going to kiss you if that's alright."

Start with a gentle kiss! I highly recommend leaving the other person wanting more. On a second date with the first partner I had after my divorce, we made out for over thirty minutes. We both loved it and just could not stop ourselves; we were both so starved for physical touch and connection.

Enjoy the foreplay, the teasing, the tempting, the wanting. With the right person, it can be a force of nature. You can tell a whole lot about your chemistry and attraction to the other person just by the nature of a kiss or foreplay intensity.

There is nothing wrong with sex on the first date, assuming you both are willing partners, and particularly if sex is all you want. (This is also assuming that you have done the necessary vetting and screening covered in previous chapters and feel absolutely safe.) "Friends with benefits" does have its...well, benefits. But like the episode from *Sex and the City*, even though Carrie's fuck buddy was great for sex, she couldn't enjoy a conversation with him, much less a date or relationship.

There's no judgment here regarding men or women who make this choice; we all have sexual needs and want to have them met. The key is to have clarity that it is *just* sex.

If you are serious about building a long-term relationship, then a hug or a kiss on the cheek or even a French kiss at the end of a date is fine, as is some casual but affectionate touching (of hands, for example) during the date if both parties are comfortable with that.

But, it can send the wrong message (for both the man and woman) to have sex on the first date while both are still unsure about the other person.

First date sex can send messages. They could include that you are promiscuous or that the physical act of sex does not mean much to you. You may send the message that you are desperate, needy, too aggressive, or lacking in self-confidence or that you will most likely have sex with your next first date, just as you did with the previous. Those messages may be completely false, but that doesn't mean they aren't being sent.

The point? Be aware, be clear, and be true to yourself.

S-E-X

For men: Yes. Simply yes. The answer to this question by men is almost always going to be *yes*, and the sooner, the better.

For women: No matter how much a woman may be physically attracted to a man, she often wonders about the right time for sex. There is no hard and fast rule; you'll have to go with whatever you feel matches your personality, your beliefs, your partner's wishes and beliefs, and the circumstances.

I often advise women that if they want to attract a quality man for a long-term relationship, do not jump into bed too soon. No matter how hot he is, how hot and bothered you are, how long it has been since your last time, or how badly you want him, *think carefully before you jump.*

Yes, men almost always want to have sex, and the sooner the better—for men, a relationship and companionship are often secondary benefits. Conversely, women want to have a relationship and companionship, but with sex as a secondary benefit. If you jump into bed with a man too early, he may not respect you. You may also not like yourself very much if you end up having an unintentional one-night stand, and you never hear back from him. (More on this in the next chapter.)

Generally, women want to warm up to a man and feel safe before having sex, but that takes time—even when there is physical attraction. Only when a woman truly trusts her partner can she fully relax and fully experience deep sexual experiences. Most women cannot orgasm if they are worried or afraid—emotions that can arise out of anything from body image issues and questions about intentions to comparison with other partners and uncertainty about perceptions.

Sexual Matching

Once you have decided to have sex, it may take a while to "get there" in terms of sexual compatibility—even if you are both highly attracted to each other.

For many, the first sexual experience with someone is often the worst. There's good news, however, and it often gets better with practice! Initially, you are just getting to know the other person and what they like or dislike. If, for example, you each prefer to be on the bottom but don't talk openly about it, both partners will become frustrated. If oral sex is a "must" for one partner and a "never" for the other, you will no doubt have problems.

But these aren't typically the matters discussed over coffee on a first date, much less on a dating profile. Once you begin to have sex with a partner, however, you can also start to openly discuss what you like and don't like. As the relationship progresses, you can continue to work on satisfying the other person and improving the sexual side of your relationship. Try a variety of different positions, places, settings, and freely share your fantasies!

If you have a high sex drive, you won't match well with someone who has a low sex drive, someone going through menopause, or someone with erectile dysfunction. Statistically, most men have a higher sex drive than women and will want and initiate sex more often, but this is certainly not always the case. I have been in the opposite situation, where the man had a much lower sex drive than me. Even after discussing my needs with him on multiple occasions, I was not satisfied. Although he was sweet and charming, our relationship didn't last.

The same principle found throughout this book applies to sex: If *you* are not right for the other person, that means *they* are not right for *you* either! Remember the funnel; continue to disqualify, disqualify, disqualify until *your* dream partner emerges.

Sexual Experience and Benefits

I strongly suggest that if it fits your values and beliefs, you should enjoy sex with multiple partners during your dating period, especially if you are just out of a long-term relationship or have not had many past sexual partners. It's important to grow yourself sexually, and to figure out what you do and do not like, and experience is the most reliable way to get there.

Plus, the rewards are worthwhile! Good sex improves your mood and overall happiness and boosts neurotransmitters, energy, and creativity. Women, in particular, want to feel connection and support with their partner (especially during ovulation). The more sex you have, the more positive hormone surges (increases in oxytocin, serotonin) and immune system benefits you get. This gets even better in a committed relationship with more frequent sex, but it also works with someone you really like and to whom you are attracted.

Safe sex is, of course, a must until you both decide to be exclusive and both have been tested for sexually transmitted diseases. There are online labs that will do local testing at a reasonable price. Don't compromise here. Sex feels better without condoms, but it's far better to practice safe sex until you *know* the relationship is exclusive than to get a disease and regret it for the rest of your life.

Exclusivity

When should you become exclusive? Some male relationship gurus suggest that men date multiple women at the same time for months on end before committing to one. I would never wait that long to be exclusive with a man, even when it's openly and honestly discussed.

It's fine, and even preferable, for both men and women *not* to be exclusive for a while—such as a few weeks—if both parties consent fully. But until you both agree openly to be exclusive, assume you are *not*, and protect yourself accordingly.

Even during a period of non-exclusivity, both men and women love to feel pursued. It makes us feel excited, appreciated, and validated, and is a huge boost to our self-esteem. After you've done your homework, your lists, your screening, your deeper screening, and made your first date assessments, give each person left standing a fair shot! Even skilled multi-taskers do not have the mental capacity to text, call, or date ten people at once. You might do that with two or three at a time, disqualify one or two along the way, and even add another one for each one you disqualify. But beyond that, you're taking energy away from pursuing what might be a long-term match.

"Next Level Dating" requires that you watch behavior over time, and disqualify those that don't fit. You can continue to screen new leads online, but by spreading yourself too thinly, you're not giving *any* partner a reasonable chance. Likewise, if you're not getting your partner's sufficient attention with the consistency of texts, calls, and in-person dates, *they* may be spread too thin dating other people.

Once you decide someone has long-term potential, and you know they feel the same way about you, I highly recommend an article from the *New York Times* that contains thirty-six questions that lead to love. Discuss these openly with your partner—you may be surprised at the answers!

If, on the other hand, you discover you and a suitor really like each other, but you don't match well romantically, consider maintaining a friendship only. I have found that most men do not want to have just friendships with women, especially those they are attracted to, but for the few who do, the relationships are golden. This is especially true when each of you is dating someone else; you can compare notes and gain valuable insights from these opposite-sex friends. I've developed several good friendships with men through my dating experiences, and my life is much richer as a result.

Introducing Kids

When should you involve your children in a dating relationship? I don't recommend it until you know with some certainty that it will be long-term. Children may suffer loss more acutely than adults, and they develop strong ties with a father or mother figure. There's no need to expose your kids to possible suffering based on a short-term relationship breakup.

Not involving kids early on has the added benefit of allowing you to build the romance, excitement, and anticipation between the two of you alone, without distractions. Even the best-behaved, lowest-maintenance kids will always be a distraction.

It is challenging, however. Kids come first, and it's difficult to find the time to discover each other and build a relationship while juggling family obligations. At least initially, schedule your dates for days or weekends when you don't have your kids or times when you can get a babysitter. If you cannot afford sitters, you may be able to spend quality time together at your place after the kids go to sleep. Sneak out during baseball practice and make out in the car. Get creative! Remember, you *need* quality time with a potential partner if you want to develop a lasting relationship.

Once you both feel sure that the other is a long-term partner, and have figured out how you would make the relationship work within a blended family, you can introduce children to the mix.

If you both have kids, introduce all of them. Plan fun activities together to slowly ease them into the new situation. A first meeting is often best done in neutral territory like a park or movie theatre, rather than one partner's home where territory and sharing issues can arise. Be sure to treat everyone equally while showing extra affection and attention.

Remember that many people are resistant to change, and kids are no different. Change can make us uneasy, guarded, or suspicious. It can also result in children testing boundaries. Don't be surprised if you experience rebellious or negative behavior from your kids or theirs. Be ready for it, and most importantly, be understanding. My daughter was an absolute brat toward my first long-term boyfriend when I introduced them. Even though she liked him, she was still extremely jealous. She called him a "mommy hogger" because she hated how much attention and affection I gave him.

I made tremendous effort to shower her with more attention and affection, but she still felt annoyed that she was no longer the only one receiving it.

This is a relationship book, not a parenting one—your situation is yours alone. Just be cautious and responsible before adding kids into the mix of your dating life for the benefit of all involved.

* * *

In the next chapter, we'll cover key issues affecting women in relationships. Men, you'll want to stick around—there's much to gain from a better understanding of women!

CHAPTER 12

For Ladies Only

Never allow someone to be your priority while allowing yourself to be their option.

-Mark Twain

Almost all the concepts in *Matched* are universal—the principles and approaches in this book will work regardless of your gender or sexual identification. Understanding what you want and taking productive steps to find it is a goal that anyone seeking a long-term relationship can identify with.

I would, however, like to devote one chapter to women—specifically to women like me, whose dream relationship is a long-term one with a quality man. (Don't worry, guys, the next chapter is dedicated to you!)

You are THE PRIZE

The single most important piece of advice for you ladies is this: *never* chase a man. *You* are the prize—so *act like it*! Behave like a selective and high-quality woman and let the man pursue you. Even if you don't believe you are the prize, act like you are until you *do*.

Don't be too easy to get; make him work for you! I don't mean playing games or *pretending* to be hard to get—I mean actually *be* hard to get. By all means, let him know that you are interested in him and excited to see him (if you are). And you can *genuinely* compliment him, too—let him know why he is special to you and why he is better than the other men you have dated. But men want and need to be the *pursuers*. Pursuit wakes the hunter instinct and makes them feel manly. Let him put the thought and effort into wooing you, into scheduling dates, into the chase.

Men appreciate you more if they need to work hard to earn your trust and love. Yes, even in our modern-day, outside the South, many men still behave chivalrously. When you let them, your value rises in a man's subconscious. You are perceived as a more valuable prize when you accept special treatment, and it makes a man feel better in your presence. I am a feminist who believes in equal rights for women, but I allow my man to open the door for me, pull out a chair for me, and carry my groceries, even though I am perfectly capable of doing those things myself. In my opinion, it enhances the male-female dynamic in the relationship.

Generally, the more time, effort, and work a man invests in the relationship, the more you mean to him, and the more likely he will be to become more personally invested in you and ultimately, to commit. But caution, ladies. In this era of online dating, men have many options, and other women are unabashed of pursuing them at the same time. Sex without effort is easier for them to come by. While you do not want to pursue, you do want to respond quickly, assertively, and enthusiastically, because if you don't, he may think you're not interested, and there may be other women chasing him.

Clues He's Into You

Women are forever trying to determine if a man we are interested in is really into us. And unfortunately, as aptly demonstrated in the movie, *He's Just Not That Into You*, we often ignore the signs that he is *not*.

Instead, we try to explain away those signs. He's not following up after a date? *He must be busy at work.* He's never asking you out on the weekend? *I realize he never told me this, but he must have his daughter every weekend.* He's never having any substantive conversation with you? *He's probably just shy.*

Women often get excited when men show them *any* interest, and we tend to make up stories about the men we like. But until proven, these stories are all in our heads, ladies! We have to verify these stories by observing a man's actions and behaviors *over time.*

Men are hunters; they *pursue* you if they are interested and will push to progress to the next steps in the relationship. You'll know it *because you will get obvious signals.* If he's into you, he'll text more often, call you more often, and schedule the next date to get closer to you as quickly as possible. He'll start blocking your "prime time" by booking dates on Friday and weekend nights so other men can't.

Conversely, if he schedules all your dates for late midweek or other inconvenient times, he's probably reserving his prime time for other women who he considers more desirable. The same applies when he texts you at 9:30 p.m. with '*Whatcha wearing, Sexy?*'

because he's bored or wants a booty call. Those aren't signs of serious pursuit.

Likewise, if a man schedules dates too far apart or at inconvenient locations for you, he's not that into you. If he is, your comfort and convenience will be important to him. If a man becomes flaky—for example, he disappears from time to time, does not respond to you in an acceptable time frame, or changes plans on you last-minute without a reasonable and believable excuse—either he's not into you, he's dating other women with more vigor, or both. They might use a technique on you called *breadcrumming,* which is contacting you from time to time with texts or calls and even scheduling dates just to keep you on a low fire as an *option* while reserving the "meat" for other women he desires more. A truly interested man will keep commitments and increase his frequency of contact. He will always be right there pursuing you.

One suitor, Jake, canceled our date at the last minute because he had to help his daughter with a school project. That was fine, but he waited more than a week before contacting me to reschedule. I politely declined, as he was clearly not that eager. Scott, on the other hand, canceled an afternoon date at the last minute because he had a board meeting that ran late. He messaged me right away and sincerely apologized. He also rescheduled the date for the next mutually available evening and sent me flowers the next day with a lovely note saying he couldn't wait to see me! Naturally, I happily obliged his request to try again.

To determine if a guy is into you, I cannot reiterate enough that you must look for clues in his *behavior* across multiple dimensions—mentally, emotionally, physically, and even spiritually. This is particularly clear in the questions he asks. A man who is into you will be curious about what makes you tick. He'll want to hear

184 | KAREN WEINSTOCK

about your family and upbringing, your friends, your education and career, and what you're passionate about. He will ask you questions about your future, what you would like to do, what activities you enjoy, what you want to accomplish in life, and more. Your Mr. Right will ask these questions because *he wants to know how to make you happy.* A quality man who is into you gets a huge natural high from pleasing you.

If you begin to open up to a man after a few dates, and he does not appear to be interested, accept it: he's probably *not* into you. But if he does appear to be interested, don't make the mistake of spilling your entire life story and opening up emotionally too soon. Don't tell him how much you like him during the first few dates—it will surely backfire and decrease his interest. Instead, maintain the mystery and keep him coming back for more. When you do begin to open up, reassess again. If he doesn't appear to be interested or engaged, he's probably not into you.

Mr. Right will be empathetic and enthusiastic about learning more about you. He will be delighted when you share your emotions with him. You have to choose a man who shows this enthusiasm, eagerness, and excitement.

One of the biggest signs that a man really *is* into you is that he will *also* open up emotionally. An interested man will share intimate things and parts of himself, including his background, beliefs, values, and spirituality. Men won't be vulnerable with women who they do not consider to be potential long-term partners.

Of course, it is equally important for you to be vulnerable as well, sharing private stories or insights such as childhood memories, passions, dilemmas, or problems you face. Once you have reached this "Next Level Dating" stage, your goal is to create intimacy in the relationship, not just lust. No long-term relationship can thrive without true intimacy, and that can only be created when you are completely yourself with another person. That is why values are so important—they provide a platform for intimacy. They allow you to dig deeper, beyond the superficial, and into the core of who you each are.

Of course, you won't find this connection with everyone, and that's fine. Don't despair if a man, even one you really like, is not into you; if you are not right for him, he most *certainly* is not right for you. His disinterest is a gift of sorts—it immediately tells you he's not a match.

You cannot manufacture compatibility. You cannot make yourself more appealing, play games, change things about yourself, and expect to increase your odds with a particular man—nor *should* you. There's a big difference between putting your best self out there (being selective in your photos, presentation, and other dating details), and trying to transform yourself to fit a mold you think a particular man wants.

Even if you temporarily "trick" a man into a relationship, it will never, ever last.

Sex (Again!)

As mentioned previously, women tend to form deeper emotional bonds and have higher expectations (and greater disappointments) after having sex with a man. Men, on the other hand, tend not to form emotional bonds right away, even after earth-shattering sex.

Ladies, if you can, remove expectations for at least a while, stop hoping that he will be "the one," and instead just fully engage in the moment. You will be much better off emotionally. Enjoy the foreplay, the sex, the closeness, and the cuddling, and limit your expectations.

The minute I learned to separate my emotions and expectations and be fully present to explore my partner and my sexuality, I became a saner person. Separating sex from emotional attachment is a skill that most men innately have. Women generally don't, but it's worth the effort to develop it—plus, it offers the bonus of keeping you from appearing needy or demanding.

For the vast majority of people, a quality romantic relationship includes a fulfilling sex life. That's why I don't worry if a man is not really into me after we have sex—his lack of interest (for whatever reason) means he wasn't a long-term match. Similarly, if I enjoy a man's company but do not enjoy sex with him, we can still be friends; it's unlikely, however, that we would ever have a successful romantic relationship.

As touched on in the prior chapter, unless you are a woman who is open to a physical relationship only, I do not advise sleeping with a man too soon. Women who rush too early into sex often have not yet built a deep emotional connection with the man. If a woman chooses to have sex before those deep emotional bonds are formed—and the choice is indeed ours, ladies—you are giving him a quick way out after he has "conquered" you. If you wait until after those initial emotional bonds are formed, however, you'll have more satisfying sex and a higher chance of a long-term match.

For a man to commit long-term to a woman, he needs a sexual connection *and* a strong enough intimacy match to let his guard down. It's this mix of sexual chemistry and emotional safety that you run the risk of unbalancing when you choose to have sex too soon, i.e., before he lets his guard down.

Many women assume that if they have a good date with a guy (and certainly once they have gone to bed with him), he will stop dating and stop sleeping with other women. *Wrong*, ladies.

In fact, making that assumption may suggest you are becoming far too emotionally committed to a guy who may or may not even want a subsequent date! Until I am sure I want to pursue a long-term relationship, I will continue to date multiple men with no exclusivity.

I can tell within a few weeks if someone has serious potential. If he does, and assuming he is continuing to pursue me, we can then discuss being exclusive. But as with everything else, this is a personal decision based on comfort level and the situation. I've had instances where a man asked me for exclusivity fairly quickly (within the second or third date), and because we were so well-matched and I did not care to date anyone else at the time, I agreed.

There are many women out there who have sex way too soon, agree to a "Friends With Benefits" arrangement, or form a casual sexual relationship with a man they want to pursue a long-term relationship with. They do so hoping that the man will fall in love with them eventually, or get used to them. Ladies, you are setting yourselves up for failure because a man who goes into a relationship with that assumption will almost never change his paradigm about what the relationship is.

Many women get hurt months and years into such an arrangement while men say: "*I was very clear from the start on what type of relationship this was.*" Women who want long-term relationships and offer sex to men way too quickly ruin it for every other woman because these men now would not be in a rush to get into a long-term relationship with *any* woman. If they can have sex so easily with women, why would they ever commit to a long-term relationship? Ladies, please think long and hard before jumping into bed with someone, make sure he is a good long-term potential for you, he actively pursues you over time, and truly invests time, effort, and money into wooing you.

My last piece of sex advice is that unless a man is impotent or has some other reason (age, medication, emotional issues) for limited interest in sex, you should assume that an active sex life is *always* going to be of importance to him. If you have low libido or know for any reason that you will not be open to an active and satisfying sex life, you should consider either doing what is necessary to increase your level of desire (consulting a medical doctor or a therapist, experimenting with things that may spark more of an interest, etc.) or disclosing your lack of interest to a potential partner early in your dating.

I have a female friend whose brother, Ritchie, has been in a very unhappy second marriage for over ten years. Ritchie is in his early sixties now and still has an incredibly strong sex drive. When he and his wife Kathy were dating, they had sex all the time. He even bragged that they had sex four times in one day.

But that was *pre*-marriage. Now, according to Ritchie, they have not had sex in over five years. Even long before that, they had stopped having actual intercourse, but she occasionally would perform a few seconds of oral sex on him, acting as if she had done him a favor. That was soon eliminated from their repertoire as well.

Clearly, Kathy either has zero sex drive, or she finds her husband undesirable—only she could answer that question. For Ritchie, however, the result is the same either way.

The moral of the story is that if your man is not being satisfied sexually by you, do *not* be surprised if he eventually turns to porn or other women. That, in fact, is precisely what Ritchie did. (A true quality man may not cheat, but instead, simply leave you, but that's of little comfort.)

All is not lost, however. A woman with a very low libido like Kathy could still match well with a man who wanted far less sex, or none at all. Everyone has a match. As always, the goal is to be clear and focused on what both of you want.

A final word on sex: whether it is important to you or not, it *is* important to the vast majority of men. You'd be wise to treat it that way—just as you might expect him to treat your birthday and anniversary as important, or to notice when you get your hair cut or wear a new dress because these things are important to *you*.

With few exceptions, sex is *very* important to him. If he's not making you want sex with him, *tell him*. I'm certain he will oblige almost any request. Better yet, you can take the lead: initiate sex and make him feel wanted and desired, which men love!

Maintain Independence, Dignity, and Boundaries (Yours *and* His)

It may sound paradoxical, but to attract a high-quality man, women must maintain their independence, and be capable of leading full and happy lives on their own. A woman who is responsible for her happiness will not be needy. You'll spark a greater desire in a high-quality man if you are happy in your freedom, but at the same time eager to add him to your life, selectively seeking his presence and intimacy. Your choice of him above any other man will endear you to him.

As the relationship moves forward, keep a full life of activities and interests apart from your man. Many women are prone to spending all their free time with their partner, which will often push him away. Don't text and talk all day long. Maintain your independence, career, family, friends, and hobbies. A high-quality woman already has a full life outside of a relationship; the right man can only enhance it.

Men seek challenges and conquests, and a high-quality woman will provide that. She will not be "easy" (sexually, or otherwise), and will demand respect. Respect is extremely important to a man. For a man to commit, he must deeply respect the woman and feel respected by her as well.

Communicate your needs without being too aggressive, nagging, or bossy; other behaviors, like blame or criticism, are unattractive and will push him away. Be assertive—know what you want and communicate your needs directly. A man must perceive you as a valuable prize in order to commit. The best way to communicate that is in what you tolerate; always maintain your dignity and self-respect.

If you have been dating for several weeks, for example, and he insists on only communicating by text, despite your stated preference for audio calls or video calls, this may be a red flag. Either he doesn't respect you, he isn't ready for commitment, he is spending time with other women, or he simply is not that into you. The reason doesn't matter; withdraw and see what happens, or just move on.

Maintaining your dignity means protecting your boundaries. Women, as a rule, are empathetic givers. We tend to want to please and are often too willing to compromise our boundaries for men. In the movie *Runaway Bride*, the character played by Julia Roberts always ordered eggs the same way her boyfriend did—she had no idea which eggs were her favorite until Richard Gere's character forced her to choose for herself. This goes beyond eggs; sometimes we make excuses for men, or convince ourselves that we can handle it, or that it's "just this once." We ask, "What if he gets mad?" or, "What if he doesn't like me if I say no?" They're all excuses for not standing strong.

When you don't resist, most men will continually push these

boundaries. Ultimately, the red lines will keep being moved and crossed until you lose your independence and sense of identity, or until you simply cannot take it anymore. Like the frog in the gradually boiling water, you don't notice the subtle changes until they've gone too far.

Statements like, "No," and "I don't like this," or, "I have a boundary about that," or, "I feel sad when you behave like this," are perfectly reasonable and *healthy* to use in a relationship. A partner who respects your boundaries and is interested in you for the long-term will understand this and will respect you *more* for assertively standing up for yourself. A man who doesn't will never be a good long-term potential match.

Stand up for yourself, or you will be pushed around until a man eventually loses respect for you—or worse, until you will lose respect for yourself.

Don't forget that you need to respect your *man's* boundaries as well. As you and your partner grow closer, you will naturally want to spend more time with him. You may feel hurt or angry if he wants to go out with his friends instead of you. But men value their independence and freedom and do *not* want to feel controlled by a woman. Rather than be hurt by this, encourage him to go out and have a good time instead. Go out yourself with your friends, have a great time, and look gorgeous while doing so.

Make sure you give your man the space he needs. Do not suffocate him or pout if he doesn't want to spend every free moment with you. That's why it's important to maintain your independence, interests, and life outside the relationship. He'll love and respect you more, and be more attracted to you because he will miss you!

Follow his Lead on Exclusivity

I advise that women wait for the man to suggest exclusivity. Similarly, I suggest that women do *not* stop dating other men—no matter how much you may like one in particular—until you have given a new partner sufficient time, *and* he has made his intention of exclusivity clear. Many men like to play the field and date multiple women at the same time. Rather than get upset, use the same strategy *yourself*—at least until you figure out if someone is worthy of your exclusivity.

As you begin your dating adventures, don't sit at home waiting for a text or call from one man; it's not a healthy strategy. While you are waiting, the man might be doing his own form of "screening" new prospects. Instead, keep your pipeline open until the relationship is more established, and both of you agree to be exclusive. Until then, assume that you are both dating other people.

Ladies, you can be eager and passionate and excited if you feel the man is equally eager and passionate and excited to pursue you. But remember that we tend to get too emotionally involved, far too quickly, before a man is ready to commit. If he tells you or indicates with his actions early on that he's not ready for a relationship, cut your losses and move on, quickly. Good men will generally tell the truth if they are not ready, or if they otherwise feel they cannot "win" in a relationship with you. Believe him when he says that he's not ready; a quality man will not want to hurt you.

Even when your man shows extreme interest in you, and you see that he's working to move the relationship forward, think long and hard about accepting exclusivity until you see consistent words and actions over time. Mr. Right will show up, will follow through on promises, and will not leave any doubt in your mind that you are important. He will be right there, texting, calling, making time for you, and being fully present. Look for consistency and congruency.

If you think a man isn't moving fast enough, do *not* push him. Some people advise women to use ultimatums to force commitment; I do not. If a man truly wants to be with you, he will find ways to be present in your life. He will consistently chase you and move the relationship forward. If you are uncertain about how he feels, try pulling back to see what happens. For example, if you usually text him back within an hour of receiving his texts, wait two or three hours, or until the next day, to respond. If he wants to schedule a date with you for Friday, cryptically say you have plans and suggest Saturday or Sunday instead.

Act less eager, be less available. Mark my words: if a man is genuinely interested in you and he even *smells* that you may still be seeing other people, he will quickly want you, the "prize," all to himself and come back running to you. If he doesn't, it means he's not that into you, so move on.

Withdraw When He Withdraws

If a man pulls away from you, it may signify that he's not that into you, has lost interest, or is just not ready for a relationship. Don't become pushy or desperate for attention. That's your anxiety and insecurity talking. Instead, pull away and give him the needed space.

If he needs some time and space to think things through, being pushy will only push him away. As above, keep him engaged, but be less available and less eager. Go on a date with someone else—it may trigger his hunter instinct or fear of losing you.

This strategy can be very effective; we all desire what we cannot have. If he pulls back, let go and pull back as well, rather than pushing into him. If he's into you, he'll come back running, and fast. He'll go overboard crazy, texting and calling more for fear of losing you to another man. Don't play games or overdo it. Mind you—if you withdraw too much, you send the message that you aren't interested. And, if you push more instead of pulling back, this sends messages of anxiety and neediness; even if he was into you, he might run faster in the other direction.

Above all, remember the *Matched* mantra: If he is just not that into you, it's better to know now and move on. Screen, disqualify, eliminate. A man who is not into you is not someone to be chased; he is someone to be *eliminated*. If you pull back and he's unaffected—meaning he also decreases contact with you or withdraws altogether—do *not* play mind games with yourself. *He's just not that into you.* Period.

Do Not Tolerate Bad Behavior

Many women who date and tolerate jerks have self-esteem problems. Unfortunately, those women ruin it for the rest of us, because men think they can get away with it. Particularly for short-term sexual relationships, many women are drawn to men who have dark personalities—issues such as narcissism, psychopathy, or Machiavellianism. Those types often show confidence, indifference, and risk-taking, or are generally more Alpha and can "sell themselves." This, however, stands in sharp contrast to what most women say they want in the long-term: a good man who is educated, successful, a loving and supportive partner, and someone who has the potential to be a good parent if there are children involved.

The truth, ladies? Good-looking men can be jerks simply because they have more options for sex. Many "bad boys" also play hard to get, and women are subconsciously (and usually temporarily) attracted to them, motivated by both the fear of loss and wanting something they cannot have.

Women need to make a conscious effort to disengage from "bad boys," particularly if their characteristics and behaviors are on the do-not-wish list, no matter *how* hot the guy is. I will never date a bad boy and will never tolerate someone who treats me badly or acts like a jerk.

Men are also notorious for treating a woman the way the woman allows them to. My fellow women, I beg of you, *do not tolerate bad behavior from a man!* If a man treats you badly, disengage, and reduce the attention you give him. Be crystal clear about what you will not tolerate. And of course, if there is too much bad behavior, break up with him.

Good behavior, on the other hand, should be reinforced. Give your man plenty of positive feedback, such as encouraging words, hugs, kisses, and other "treats." Unless you are dealing with a narcissist or psychopath, positive reinforcement works like a charm with children *and* men—and us women as well!

Listen to Your Intuition

If your gut is telling you that something is wrong, it often is.

There is much truth in the idea that our "fast" brain (or "system one" as the brilliant Daniel Kahneman calls it in his book *Thinking Fast and Slow*) can make a decision in a split second. Our thinking brain (or "system two") will take much more energy and time to process decisions. It is a combination of the two systems that works best.

Women's intuition is usually better than men's, but because many women get too emotionally engaged, they neglect to (or intentionally do not) check their instincts.

I dated a man who checked almost every box in my wish list, with no apparent downside. He was charming and intelligent and seemed to do everything right. My paradigm is "trust but verify"— to believe what the other person says but always check their words against objective facts. I prefer this to being overly suspicious, which is neither fun nor a healthy way to live life or enter into a relationship.

When mister near-perfect told me a few things that I found hard to believe rationally, I also felt a physical reaction in my gut. Since my intuition had never failed me, I was sure he was lying.

I checked the facts, and sure enough, my gut was correct. I broke the relationship off quickly, knowing I would never be able to trust him.

Don't Obsess about *Why*

While men generally have the biological and psychological drive to connect with others, to find love, and to reproduce, they usually don't sweat it as much if a date or a relationship goes wrong. They just move on to the next person. While I certainly appreciate thoughtful analysis and introspection after a date, I don't believe in ripping yourself apart after a bad date. The same applies to a seemingly good one after which he never calls again. Dwelling on things too long never helps.

When I was new to dating and never heard back from a guy after what I thought was a good date, I questioned myself. *What had I done wrong? Why didn't he like me?*

These are the wrong questions to ask. Self-reflection is good. It can be helpful to analyze whether you presented your true and best self. But it's not useful to engage in self-deprecating behavior and obsessing over *why*. A failed date doesn't mean there is anything "wrong" with you or how you behaved. If you were your authentic self, and there was no match, that's perfectly okay. The *why* is not important.

Instead of asking why he behaved a certain way, why he never called back, or what you did wrong, ask yourself what you *learned* from that experience. Did you gain an insight into yourself or the dating process that can help in the future? Take note, then bring closure to the relationship and move on.

Elevate his Feelings of Manliness

A man needs to pursue, lead, protect, and provide; *let* him. Allowing him to do "manly" things for you increases his testosterone, which in turn boosts his happiness, sex drive, confidence, and attraction to you. Asking a man to do you a favor usually makes him like you more than if you had done the favor for *him*!

A woman should encourage a man's dreams and ambitions and make him feel respected, admired, confident, and appreciated. While most women crave love and attention, most men want to be respected and admired. Giving a man a thoughtful and genuine compliment will boost his confidence and endear you to him; just make sure it is honest and well-deserved. Speak positively about him to other people to boost his self-esteem. Support your man in what he does, and be enthusiastic about his dreams and passions. If you feel true appreciation and admiration for something he did or is, tell him.

One of the great powers of femininity is in being able to attract help and support—accepting that help elevates the man who provides it. The deepest and most important expression of that is for a woman to activate a man's hero instinct, allowing a man to feel worthy by engaging in a heroic act. Accomplishing the mission can cut through a man's emotional walls—whether that mission is achieving a goal, protecting someone, or earning respect.

A quality man should get a natural high from meeting your needs. He should feel *good* when he makes you happy and fulfills your dreams, so create opportunities for him to do so, and then show appreciation when he does. Remember that it's easier for a man to help you to solve problems that have physical or concrete solutions (like killing a spider or fixing a door). This not only raises the man's testosterone levels and feelings of manliness, but it also elevates your estrogen levels to ask for and receive help, and to feel you are in a safe environment.

Ladies, give your men concrete directions to do things for you. Tell him how he can please and help you. When you tell him you appreciate him and that he's your hero, then he will be!

CHAPTER 13

Good Guys, Bad Boys

Every boy wants a good girl to be bad just for him.
Every girl wants a bad boy to be good just for her.

-Unknown

While men and women have very different needs at the start of a relationship, those needs converge over time. Deep down, both want companionship, connection, and intimacy. We all hope for respect, mutual support, and affirmation of our desirability.

How we get there, however, can be very different. The previous chapter offered advice specifically to women; this one will focus on men. The pages ahead will help quality men find and establish better long-term relationships with well-matched partners. (And ladies, do not skip this chapter, as it has important insights for you as well.)

Most women who are looking for a long-term relationship really *do* want to end up with nice, solid guys. The problem is that far too many of those solid men miss the mark and send women running to the bad boys. Many times, the good guys behave in ways that don't attract women or send mixed messages. It's time to put a stop to that.

The Hook

A long-term relationship must start with a hook of attraction—a genuine seed of interest from both sides. But those hooks are different for men and women.

Men initially tend to focus more on physical aspects such as appearance, touching, kissing, and having sex *because that is the primary way that men connect with women*. The most important advice I have for guys is: *do not go for chemistry first*. Don't write on your profile "chemistry first, let's go out for drinks." Women want emotional support and connection. They want to develop trust with a man first before they feel comfortable enough to fully connect physically. For men, an emotional connection without physical connection is meaningless and empty. Not necessarily so for women; we can have girlfriends and gay friends to gossip with and do other "female" activities. A surefire way to get most men to run is to invite them shoe shopping. A surefire way to get most women to run is to leap directly to sex as quickly as possible.

A woman can set the hook with a man she likes by conveying sexual availability—in the way she dresses, flirts, smiles, touches her body and hair, talks, and carries herself. But for men, it's a little more complicated. The hooks that follow will help you, the good guys, to up your game.

Build Yourself Up

Bad boys are great at creating an attractive profile that tells everyone how great they are—they're experts at the hook. For good guys, writing a great profile seems far more difficult.

It's time to get comfortable with tooting your own horn. Write down your best attributes and why you are a good catch for the type of quality woman you seek. Tell us how great you are, how important you are, and all about your professional or personal accomplishments. Get over your self-conscious self and make her want you more. Give her a reason to swipe right!

Don't brag too much or over-inflate. If you struggle to find the right balance, have your best friends validate or help you write your profile.

Appearance

Pay close attention to your appearance. Just as her appearance is important to you, yours matters as well.

Part of the reason women are attracted to bad boys is that they at least make an effort to look good. Many will dedicate time and effort to staying in shape and dressing well. Even if their goal is only sex, they've still made an effort, and it shows.

Men prefer women who are in shape, have a nice physique, and look feminine and attractive. Women want you to look attractive, too.

I once had a first date with an otherwise nice guy who wore sweat pants and a baseball cap. Not only was it a complete turn-off for me that he didn't make an effort to look halfway decent, but the cap covered his head and hair and most of his face. I couldn't even tell if I found him attractive!

Initial attraction is just as important to women as it is to you. It doesn't matter if you have movie star looks—make an *effort*. Even if a woman is not initially totally attracted to you, your other good qualities can make a difference. But don't lose before you start by not at least trying.

Make Your Move

When men come on too strong, too soon, they can be perceived by women as being too aggressive, too sex-driven, or just plain jerks. Unlike men, most women need to develop trust to go to bed.

Nice guys know this, and it makes them hesitant to make *any* move. They wait to engage in even the slightest touch, like briefly holding a woman's hand, much less an intimate hug or kiss because they want to be perceived as nice, respectful, and not too aggressive. The problem is that this may send the message to the woman that you are not interested in her romantically or sexually, and she may move you into the "friend zone," unsure of where things stand.

Conversely, more aggressive men and bad boys don't hesitate to make a move when they are interested, particularly when they are getting a clear message from her. They often don't care if they come across as assholes; if they strike out, they simply move on to the next woman. Good guys, on the other hand, who are worried about perception or rejection tend to wait to make a move until they feel sure. For you nice guys, this can be the dating kiss of death.

I had a first date with a truly nice guy, and I was definitely attracted to him. At the end of the date, he gave me a friendly hug like you might give an acquaintance. After a great second date, he still didn't make a move to kiss me. We stood near my car, with me about to move him to the friend zone and drive off, when he mentioned that he really wanted to kiss me but wasn't sure if I wanted him to. I immediately said, "Would you please kiss me already?" and leaned into him. We kissed for ten phenomenal and sensual minutes—an opportunity that was almost lost because he did not make a move that would let me know he was interested in me romantically.

Gentlemen, if you are interested in a woman romantically, make a move of some kind, and make it fast. Touch a woman's hand gently during your first date. Place your hand on the small of her back when you walk her to the car. Help her put on her coat, hug her closely, give her a soft kiss on the cheek, and, if the moment seems right, just ask permission to kiss her.

If you are asking, you probably already have a good idea that she wants you to. If she declines at first, however, but accepts another date, you still have another chance; she may just be moving more slowly than you. On the other hand, if she says no and you feel like she is just not interested, accept the rejection and move on. Remember, if *you* are not the one for her, then *she* is not the one for you either! Don't feel "less than" or question what is "wrong" with you. Simply be thankful you have eliminated yet another mismatch and are now one step closer to Ms. Right.

Romance and Passion

You nice guys may think you're being romantic, but *nice* and *romantic* are not the same thing. Instead of bringing the passion and mystery to the pursuit, you can be predictable (boring) or act too sweetly, with none of the passion and excitement that leaves us wanting more. Acting in ways that are caring, sweet, and loving is extremely important, but we ladies also need a sense of excitement, mystery, and romance. We enjoy being chased and adored. Without passion and excitement, chemistry is difficult to build, and you may find yourself in the friend zone.

Some bad boys *act* like nice guys but really are *not*. They use women by being nice to them to get something that they want (sex, often, but also affection and even love). Please don't be *that* douchebag! (It's not lost on me that the bad boys and douchebags are most

204 | KAREN WEINSTOCK

likely *not* reading this book!) If you are truly interested in her for the long-term, pursue her a little more passionately. Respect her boundaries, of course, but pursue her, and don't act disinterested or play hard-to-get. Text her. Call her. Schedule more in-person dates. Engage with her in deeper conversations. Bring or send flowers and thoughtful gifts—they don't have to be expensive; they simply let her know you appreciate her. All these things increase intimacy and emotional connection with the woman you are pursuing.

Appreciation and Attention

Being appreciated is one of the most important things for a woman in a romantic relationship. Value her for who she is, for her genuine nice qualities, and for what she does for you and others. Find ways to appreciate her each day and tell her about it. It will enhance her feelings towards you tenfold.

Women need to feel *heard*. Listen to her, actively, even if all she wants to do is vent. When men talk and ask questions, it is usually to solve a problem. When women talk, they often just want to be heard and validated. They want to rehash something, share what they are feeling, or talk about their day.

That sharing needs to happen in a safe environment. Let her share openly and just actively listen. Do not try to solve any problems or give advice unless she *specifically* asks. Just mirror her, acknowledging what she said and how she's feeling. For example: "You are perfectly justified in being pissed at Emily. I can't believe she talked to you like that in front of your boss. No wonder you're so upset."

Attention and appreciation can take other forms, too. If your lady asks for help with something within reason—like painting the bathroom or having the oil changed in her car—be her hero! You will both feel better. She'll feel loved, supported, and appreciated, and you'll get the "hero high!"

Intimacy and Emotional Connection

Men, of course, aren't *entirely* different from women. You, too, may have found yourself feeling empty after a one-night stand. Whether you admit it or not, you also crave intimacy and want a partner you can be your authentic self with.

One-night stands are not an adequate substitute for intimacy. *Real* intimacy and emotional connection aren't just about sex (although that is certainly important), it's about letting your guard down and sharing your inner fears and insecurities and who you are deep down inside. When you do, and a woman responds with compassion and shares as well, you feel secure and connected. The combination of vulnerability and compassion on both sides is what leads to lasting connection and love.

Men often resist opening themselves up emotionally because it makes them vulnerable. You may view that as a dangerous thing because you have:

- a fear of being hurt or manipulated by a woman because you have been hurt before.
- a fear of appearing weak to a woman you like or are trying to impress.
- a fear that an emotionally vulnerable man will be dropped into the friend category.

Many men have also been taught by their parents to "man up," or that "boys don't cry"—sentiments that unfortunately reinforce for men that being vulnerable is a bad thing. Society, too, teaches that emotions such as fear or sadness or insecurity are not manly. This is the reason why many men develop defense mechanisms or wear "masks" to protect themselves from *any* feelings, much less difficult ones such as shame or rejection.

It's not an effective strategy to run from your emotions and stay disconnected from the person you really are. You run the risk of living your entire life with low emotional intelligence, which can have far-reaching effects in all your relationships. You have a much better chance of genuinely hooking a quality woman by being emotionally available and vulnerable. Share personal and intimate details about your life. Tell her about your passions, hobbies, beliefs, values, and spirituality. It is a risk worth taking—it will convey emotional openness to a woman, which she will both value and return in kind.

You don't need to share your entire life history and vulnerabilities with a woman early on—not until some level of trust is built—but emotional openness will score high points with a woman. It sends the signal that you are interested and that you can be yourself, open up, and share.

Take the risk. Even if you've been hurt before, a lack of vulnerability or compassion for her will stop you from establishing an intimate connection. Emotionally intelligent men know they don't have to be a rock of emotional fortitude 24/7. They can feel and show difficult emotions, be open and vulnerable, and share their fears and insecurities with the right woman. Open up emotionally and be vulnerable—it's the path to winning her trust, and eventually, her heart.

Social Distancing

Dating during social distancing can aid in building better connections and intimacy. I am grateful that I was able to experience dating in a whole new era of social distancing and stay-at-home quarantine orders during the COVID-19 epidemic. It has been an unprecedented time of physical distancing and social isolation.

Staying six feet apart from others and avoiding meeting people in person isn't what most people would call a great dating environment. You lose the ability to connect with your partner in person and become more reliant on photos, swipes, and online profiles. When no true connections are made, feelings of loneliness, depression, and anxiety increase. For men, testosterone levels can plummet in fight or flight mode.

Still, I believe that social distancing has been a good thing for many people seeking long-term partners. The pandemic has forced many to take things slower, building deeper emotional connections first and delaying in-person dates until much later.

This "dating from a distance" forces both men and women to open up and have extended and deeper conversations with their potential matches. There's more time to explore potential partners and whether they may be a good fit. It also lets searchers explore what they like without the complications of chemistry that come from jumping into a physical relationship early.

And (guys!) yes, a level of intimacy is possible without meeting in person. I had long phone calls and video calls with potential partners during the two months I was forced to stay at home, and I gained one romantic relationship and two friends. I was also able to weed out liars quicker, for example, those who couldn't go on a call or video chat because they were living with someone else. And,

I was able to find creative ways to go on physical dates—taking a walk in a nature trail, for example, which was lovely and allowed me to connect with my date on a deeper level.

Pandemic or not, time and distance are a chance to slowly build an emotional connection that you will both benefit from instead of meeting too quickly before you have barely scratched the surface in getting to know them.

The Story of My "Don Juan"

This true story from my dating experience fits the intent of this chapter and can help good guys understand how to pursue a quality woman. It's also a lesson for men on how *not* to act, and a good lesson for women, too.

I matched with Don on Tinder because of his interesting profile. He was an entrepreneur and inventor, and a successful creative director in his own company. He wrote that he was interested in meeting driven, intelligent, articulate women who have a passion for experiencing life.

Bingo! I thought. *A perfect initial match—my ideal profile, exactly.* He also mentioned that he was interested in a long-term relationship with the right woman, and in building an authentic relationship instead of one-night stands. *Double bingo!* The only drawback was that he had four children, but if he was the right guy for me, I knew I was willing to try to make it work.

Don and I chatted online, and the conversation flowed easily. He was articulate, intelligent, and funny. Few of my chats in the past had gone as deep as our initial conversation did. He volunteered that he had been married for fourteen years, divorced for three, and that his four children were close in age to my daughter. He had just joined Tinder but felt a little awkward because he wasn't interested in hook-ups or empty conversations.

I soon discovered that Don's flexible custody schedule would likely work with mine. *Another bingo!* He gave me his full name and phone number, and after some online digging, I felt comfortable enough to give him mine as well. He was Canadian, another bonus for me because they are generally easygoing and have a cute accent.

We texted back and forth that first evening, and then he just called out of the blue. It was a pleasant surprise since I was home alone during the pandemic, and my daughter was with her dad for the weekend. I liked Don's deep baritone voice, and he was as charming, funny, and easygoing on the phone as he was in texting.

Don commented again that he liked to have fun but was not interested in games. He asked me some probing questions to get to know me, and I did the same; we wasted little time on small talk. The conversation flowed easily from both sides, and almost two hours later, we said goodnight. It felt like only minutes had passed, and I liked his energy, intelligence, charm, and how funny he was.

Over the next couple of days, Don and I continued to text and have long phone calls, eventually progressing to FaceTime. Our conversations were effortless, funny, and pleasant. He seemed genuinely interested in intimacy, and shared much about his past, including some vulnerabilities about his upbringing. He asked me many of the right questions about likes and dislikes, about love languages, and expressed how he liked to connect and build intimacy in a relationship. We had both traveled internationally and had dozens of countries under our belts, and we talked about those experiences along with things we would like to do in the future. He also liked to ski with his kids. The bingos kept rolling in.

Don continued to text and call me with just the right frequency.

He paid me nice compliments like, *I enjoyed our conversation this morning,* and *loved hearing your laugh. Looking forward to talking later.* He called once or twice a day "just to hear my voice," and kept telling me how he enjoyed our conversations, how I made him laugh, and how he wanted to meet me in person soon. He once sent a text that said: *My thoughts have drifted to you throughout the day Karen and have made me smile. Thought I would share vs. it just being in my head.*

All of it demonstrated to me that this man was very much interested in me, but also that he was confident enough in himself to be vulnerable and emotionally open with me—a big turn-on for any woman!

As time passed, I learned more and more about Don. He checked almost every box on my wish list and didn't appear to check any at all in the do-not-wish department. He called me when he said he was going to and texted me when he could not—he was congruent with his actions. He often sent funny texts, such as: *At least you think I'm amusing. It will wear on you.* He had a sense of humor and could laugh at himself.

As time went on, Don progressed with his texts, sending things like:

… I do love your laugh, even when it's at your own joke

… I would love to kiss you

… You can tell a lot about our chemistry just by our kiss

… The meeting of 2 personalities is like the contact of 2 chemical substances: if there is any reaction, both are transformed. (Carl Gustave Jung).

When I texted him that my daughter was not happy being home during the pandemic, he replied with kid jokes to cheer her up. When I could not talk or text because I was spending time with her, he would say, 'No worries! She's the priority.'

Let's pause the story. This is a good time to take notes from Don as a good example of how a man who is truly interested in a woman would actively pursue her. His efforts cost nothing more than time and thoughtfulness. Note, ladies, that I was not pursuing him, but just responding considerately and thoughtfully with texts like I love the quote. I am hopeful for chemistry when we meet in person.

At some point, Don asked if I liked poetry, and began to send me beautiful poems, some from famous romantic poets, and some he wrote himself. He openly shared not just how much he liked me, but what he liked about me—my smile, our diverse and easy conversations, and that he thought I was amazingly beautiful. He was not shy or insecure about his feelings.

After we had been talking about a week, Don recommended meeting in person. We both knew it would be easier to see in person if we had chemistry; if we didn't, then we could move on. For quarantine reasons, we decided it was best to meet outside.

Before the date, he texted: Thinking about you... not to be too distracting ... rather to know that I'm making you smile. Perhaps making you blush as I imagine tracing my lips down your neck. Taking you in as I hold you close. Very forward, yet romantic and not too aggressive.

I was not disappointed. I already knew what he looked like from our video chats, but Don was even better looking and more charming in person, and his 6'4" height and muscular body only added to the appeal. He had built up the sexual tension ahead of the date, and when he said that he was dying to kiss me and could not wait any longer, neither could I.

It was one of the best first dates I'd ever had. We had developed a strong connection and even some intimacy ahead of time. Don was respectful, gentle, assertive, and a great kisser, and we had great chemistry, as I had hoped. Don's energy was incredible with mine. (The lesson? Don't be afraid to take charge, gentlemen. Make your move. Be bold. The worst thing that can happen is that she says *no*. That, I can assure you, is less painful than regret.)

After our initial meeting, Don continued to text and call me, but now with more frequency and vigor. We planned our next date, this time for him to come to my home. We had a lovely dinner, conversation, and more foreplay—the fireworks continued.

Don suggested that on my next free weekend, we should go to an Airbnb in Tennessee where there was no quarantine. Part of me felt it was too early for a weekend getaway—we'd only started the relationship a couple of weeks earlier—but after more than a month stuck at home, I needed a getaway.

Although I broke my own rules—to not go away with someone too early or have sex too soon—I knew full well what I was doing. I just wanted to enjoy the weekend and be present with him. And I was right—the weekend was magical. We had spent some time alone together already, and I trusted that Don would not hurt me. He had been gentle and respected my boundaries, and we had even already agreed to exclusivity. Don had been texting me almost every morning and night, and multiple times during the day. We were both busy with work, but we still made time for quality communication. The frequency and quality of texts and phone calls and the one-on-one time we had spent together made me confident he was very much exclusively into me.

Don continued to up the romance factor (take note, gentlemen). He booked the vacation, picked me up, carried my luggage, and even made sure we had drinks and snacks for the road. We made out for a little while before we left, and then again when we stopped for gas and groceries.

Don paid for everything. He opened the car door for me, carried everything into the house he had rented, and brought several special items with him to up the romance, including a Bluetooth speaker, candles, and bath salts. He played Sinatra, we danced close, and we enjoyed lots of foreplay and great sex.

The intimacy between us grew as we cuddled, talking about our pasts and our aspirations for the future. Don drew me a bath that we both soaked in for an hour and talked while he rubbed my back and shoulders. We went out to dinner, on a romantic walk, and for an excursion on a private riverboat.

At some point, the intensity of the romance Don showered me with over the weekend did raise the suspicion that he was a player. But, I reminded myself, he had been married for fourteen years; he was clearly capable of committing to the right woman. Plus, I still had not seen any deal breakers in his behavior, or anything that would bother me much. (He did snore, but that is fixable!) I can usually identify fairly quickly what traits in a potential partner are not desirable to me, but Don seemed to be a perfect match. Despite my gut concerns, I continued forward, determined to simply enjoy the time together.

When Don and I had been dating for about a month, two issues needed resolution. The first was that he had yet to invite me to his place. The second was that I had never met his children or seen what kind of father he was.

I had plenty of patience for the latter—meeting kids is best done once a relationship is well-established—but I had a bigger problem with the former. Why wasn't I being invited to his home?

I asked Don to meet at his place for our next date. Although he said yes initially, he made a last-minute excuse about why we couldn't. We rescheduled, and he dodged a visit to his place again. The excuses mattered less than the last-minute cancellation pattern—it's a clear red flag in a growing relationship, and so is not being invited to your partner's place. Yes, there were many potentially harmless reasons, but the last-minute change had put me on alert.

Our next child-free weekend together, Don and I again planned to spend time at his home. The day before, he revealed that he had to fly to California for an emergency investor meeting his partner had arranged. I didn't argue with that excuse, but my gut told me Don was lying. I played along, though, and asked him to let me know how his trip went. In the meantime, I intended to find out the truth.

Since I now had unplanned free time with my daughter away, I began to look into what Don had told me, digging into public records and social media posts. When I contacted the realtor who was listing his house, there it was: a few months prior, Don had moved back to his ex-wife's home.

I considered the options. Best case scenario, Don's move was for financial reasons that he was embarrassed to tell me about (which could have been understandable, especially for a strong, successful man). Worst case scenario, they were back together. Either way, he had lied to me.

I immediately knew I was likely going to have to end the relationship either way, and I began to detach emotionally. Rather than immediately judging him harshly based on the little information I had, I wanted to be compassionate, give him a chance to explain himself, apologize if appropriate, and to allow him to get out with dignity and grace. I did want to try and give him the benefit of the doubt. I couldn't deny that I liked him a lot, and he had treated me very well over the weeks we had been dating. But regardless of the truth, I needed closure.

I knew by this point that pushing Don to go to his place would lead nowhere, so I invited him to my place during an afternoon when my daughter was out. He immediately agreed and came in the door smiling and happy to see me. After a quick hug and kiss, I asked him to sit down and told him that before we went any further, there was something that I wanted to clear up.

If he was worried, he hid it well. I dove right in. "I know you lied to me about the business trip to California," I said. "I just want to know *why* you lied." Before he could say anything, I assured him I wouldn't be angry, but that if he was not completely honest with me, our relationship could not continue. A look of complete shock came across Don's face, and he said, "I did *not* lie to you about my business trip. I *did* go to California to meet with the investors."

Before Don could continue lying, I interjected that I knew California was still under a strict shelter-in-place order, and that no one, much less astute business people, would demand a face-to-face meeting that also required air travel. Don protested further, insisting that he *did* fly to California on business. I then asked him to show proof of his plane ticket. He fumbled and scrolled on his phone, then eventually mumbled that it must be on his desktop. I asked him that if he couldn't find the email containing the ticket, he could show me proof from his credit card statement. There was silence. After a moment, I asked again, "Why did you lie to me about going to California?" This time he replied truthfully: "Because I didn't want you to come to my place."

Don then proceeded to weave a story about living in a friend's basement because he was doing renovations to his house to prepare it for sale. This would have been perfectly believable if it had been the truth, but he neglected to mention anything about moving in with his ex-wife.

When I told him I had spoken with the realtor and knew he did not even own the house, but had rented it before the renovations started, Don quit speaking altogether and simply stared out the patio door. He had begun to sweat profusely, and his hazel eyes were dilated and dark. I calmly told him that I never wanted to see or hear from him again, that I suspected he was narcissistic and should consider getting some help, especially for the sake of his children. I then thanked him for making the break-up so easy for me. After a pause, Don stood up, leaned down, and kissed me gently on the lips as if to say, *Touché, you got me*, and walked out the door.

It was the easiest break-up of my life. I didn't hesitate or second-guess the decision. I knew I was doing the right thing for *me*. Had we stayed together, he would have continued to lie and manipulate me and would have eventually crossed my boundaries. I was thankful to have identified early on that he was incapable of ever loving me. I didn't feel sad but *empowered*.

Don was indeed incredibly romantic. For a period of time, he swept me off my feet. But it was unsustainable because it wasn't *real*. For you quality men seeking quality women, remember to be real and do right by the women you date. Once you find a woman you like, take a break from chasing other women at the same time, and focus on her. Be thoughtful, be romantic, and be interested. But above all else, be *true*. It will pay off in the long run.

CHAPTER 14

Why Relationships Fail

The course of true love never did run smooth.

-William Shakespeare

Let's face it. Any relationship between two people is hard to maintain for a prolonged period. In our tribal past, the family unit was larger. The entire tribe or village took care of kids collectively, gathered food collectively, and cooked collectively. There was little expectation that one individual would do everything for the family.

In modern times, tribal life has changed. Often, both partners work *and* take care of the household, and there can be much pressure on one or both partners to fulfill all the needs of the other, ranging from food and shelter to child care and emotional comfort.

It's vital that we recognize that most of us are not built for that; each person must keep their independence in a relationship. This includes being your own person, having your own interests and friends, and spending time away from each other to renew your energy.

Still, despite all our best efforts, most relationships fail. Why?

Lack of Common Values and Beliefs

Attraction and great sex are important in a romantic relationship. Without them, the chemical mix of oxytocin, dopamine, and other love hormones would not be there to bind you.

The trouble, however, is that these love hormones can make you feel so good that they temporarily blind you to your partner's negative qualities. After the initial infatuation stage, when the hormones begin to fade, you both begin to see your respective imperfections, which are often too great for the relationship to last.

The *Matched* process works to prevent that by asking you to select the qualities, values, and beliefs you want in a partner *first*, and then actively looking for someone who possesses them. Only then do you look for chemistry and begin to build an intimate, quality relationship.

This approach of compatibility before chemistry gives you much better odds of finding a long-term life partner who is best suited for *you*. When you begin with the end in mind, instead of jumping in too quickly, your chances of success are much higher.

Complacency

At the beginning of a relationship, we will romance, pursue, excite, thrill, charm, and do whatever it takes to win another's heart. We put our best foot forward, changing behaviors and habits, and making the extra effort. But as the relationship matures, we become used to each other, and the romance slips away. In the long run, many relationships fade, simply because we take the other person for granted and get used to the status quo. Performance expert Tony Robbins notes that people don't do at the end of a relationship the same beautiful and thoughtful things they did at the beginning. Many relationships die a long and painful death as behaviors shift over time from loving and pleasing the other to self-absorption and negativity.

Partly to blame is our hedonic adaptation mechanism, that part of our brain that makes us return to a stable level of happiness (or, for some, unhappiness), despite major positive or negative life effects. We think the bigger house will make us happier, so we buy it. A few months later, the excitement fades, we get used to our bigger house, and we wind up just as happy as we were in the old one.

Relationships are similar, and it takes thought, effort, and action to avoid both the steady decay and the mistaken desire for an unneeded "upgrade."

To prevent this from happening, make a *daily* habit of appreciating your partner. Thank them for something that they do, or for a quality you admire. Each time you stop to feel and share gratitude for your partner, you fight and win the war against complacency.

Quality time helps win the war, too—schedule date nights away from the house and the day-to-day hustle at least once a week. Even a small romantic getaway like spending the night at a hotel in town, just the two of you, will reap great happiness rewards. Connect physically and emotionally. You don't need to go on an overseas trip for two weeks to avoid complacency; just make it a weekly habit to spend quality time together.

Disagreements

Contrary to common belief, many relationships fail not because of arguments, or even what the arguments are *about*. It's *how* you argue with your partner and *how you resolve* disagreements that matter. The process is more predictive of relationship quality than anything else.

Look for behavioral patterns when you fight or disagree. Do you respect each other and resolve things through honest and open communication and feedback? Are there red flags in the other person's behavior that trigger you? One of my ex-husband's traits during arguing was to argue to exhaustion if necessary. He *always* needed to be right. From my perspective, he never tried to truly understand me, hear me, consider my viewpoint, or validate my feelings. Instead, he attacked like a bulldog, criticizing me and depleting me emotionally until I no longer had the energy to keep arguing.

Over time, I learned to bottle up things that were bothering me simply to avoid an argument. This was, of course, a double-edged sword. My resentment grew like a snowball until I just could not take it anymore, and then it exploded into an avalanche.

The bright side? I learned to immediately voice my opinion and talk about things that bother me. It was a good life lesson to learn that the right partner would listen and try to understand me.

Disagreements, and even fights, can be healthy for a relationship and are inevitable if both people are honest and authentic. How you *resolve* those disagreements will be indicative of how good your communication is, and how successful your relationship has the potential to be.

If you never disagree with your partner, don't fool yourself that things are perfect. You either are dating yourself, stuck in a shallow relationship, or one (or both) of you is not being honest or authentic and is instead sweeping things under the rug.

My marriage counselor told me that during a conflict, each person needs to think about the conflict from the other person's perspective at the same time they are thinking about their own. In addition to the two points of view, imagine there is a third—a marriage therapist in the room evaluating each viewpoint and giving advice. What would the therapist say in this situation? What kinds of solutions would the therapist recommend? What kinds of conclusions did both of you come to?

Whatever you do during a disagreement, never use the silent treatment, stonewalling, or ostracism. Silence, withdrawal, and sulking are unproductive and can become abusive, controlling behaviors that many passive-aggressive and narcissistic personalities use to manipulate or punish their partner.

For even a well-meaning person, refusing to engage or communicate is an unhealthy coping mechanism. You may see it as an effort to gain self-control, take the high road, handle the situation "rationally," or simply avoid conflict, but silence resolves very little. It's an unhealthy way to communicate displeasure, anger, frustration, and pain.

Regardless of the reason behind it, expect resentment and the deterioration of the relationship. The silent treatment, the ostracism, the stonewalling—they all cause emotional pain, which activates the same parts of your brain as physical pain does. The ostracized person is denied basic human emotional needs and can feel lonely, depressed, anxious, and stuck, wondering what they did wrong, and when it will end.

For the passive-aggressive or narcissistic type, ostracizing is an intentional form of emotional abuse. It's also a control mechanism—after all, you cannot argue with someone who won't speak to you. They decide when to break the silence treatment, which can last for hours, days, or even weeks while they enjoy how the other person suffers and pleads with them to break the silence.

The abusers punish by refusing to speak to their victims who are left isolated, uncertain when or if the silence will be broken.

Toxic Personalities

I had a friend once who said, "All women are crazy. All men are stupid." Amusing, and there is no doubt that relationships can be unhealthy for a myriad of reasons that are certainly not gender-specific. I would like to focus on narcissistic personalities, however, which statistically are more likely to be in men. Narcissism (a term which I will generally use to also describe those who are psychopaths or have other issues such as borderline disorder) is particularly toxic to relationships, all the more so because we are all selfish and self-absorbed at times and it can be so difficult to spot.

It seems counterintuitive, but many smart and successful women end up in toxic relationships. Women are often drawn to the darker male personalities—an Alpha male, perhaps, who is attractive, exciting, charming, intelligent, self-confident, and ambitious. The chemistry and sex are incredible too, and his initial attention and perceived devotion provide a chemical high that's easy to fall for.

The flip side, however, is much darker. Other narcissistic traits include self-absorption, entitlement, vanity, selfishness, superiority, and an excessive need for admiration with no ability to tolerate criticism. Narcissists have a disregard for feelings and will exploit others as objects for their own gain.

Deep down, the narcissist's confidence, sense of entitlement, and feelings of superiority are, in reality, a psychological façade to defend against their very fragile ego and true feelings of insecurity, inadequacy, inferiority, and even shame when feeling exposed and vulnerable.

Remember Don Juan from the previous chapter? I had never dated someone before that I (later) suspected was a narcissist. I discovered that early on in a relationship, narcissists present themselves as loving, helpful, considerate, and romantic. They act like the perfect mate, and adore a woman, showering her with gifts, good sex, and "love" (a true narcissist is not capable of the real thing). This technique is called *love bombing*, and it's used to lure victims to fall in love or come to depend upon the narcissist, until they later reveal their true colors and things turn ugly.

Love bombing is often difficult to detect. Being showered with affection, admiration, and gifts can be extremely exciting at the start of a new relationship and create a natural high. With love bombing, the perpetrator overwhelms his victim with loving words, actions, and gifts, thereby winning her trust and gaining control.

Love bombing is easier to detect when it's over the top—receiving five bouquets rather than one, or a very expensive piece of jewelry right at the beginning of a relationship. It can also be overly intense—too many texts, phone calls, and date requests as the narcissist tries to monopolize time and attention.

Don's love bombing was moderate and believable. His poetry and how much he said he adored me were a little much, but he had a creative brilliance and a stated romantic streak, so I accepted it. He played the part of the pursuer perfectly.

Love bombing not only effectively lures the victim, but it also helps narcissists build themselves up as the perfect partners to satisfy their own needs for admiration, connection, and power. It helps them shape their victim to act the way they want, and they may withdraw that affection later if the victim does not behave accordingly. Had I not remained at least somewhat emotionally disengaged, I would definitely have fallen in love with him during the love-bombing stage, and the break-up would have been difficult.

Watch for phrases like *you're perfect,* or *I only want to spend time with you,* as they could be red flags early on in a relationship. During our courtship, Don could not name one thing that he did not like about me when I asked. I jokingly said, "Just give it time," and left it there.

Another red flag is becoming angry when they are not the exclusive focus of your attention. Narcissists will want to rush things, make big plans for the future early on, such as moving in together. Don offered exclusivity fairly quickly, but I assumed it was because he knew what he wanted and went after it. It's an Alpha quality I like, but also a common control tactic for narcissists.

Later in the relationship, a narcissist will try to shape their partner to be their "supporting cast." Since they perceive themselves as better than others, they can't have equal and mutually satisfying relationships. Instead, they limit their partner's time with friends or in activities that do not include them. Ladies, be especially alert to this type of behavior. A man who truly cares about you will support your time apart and encourage your hobbies and time spent with your friends and family.

Once their true colors are revealed, narcissist relationships quickly turn sour. They devalue their partners, blame, call names, and do anything to maintain control. This keeps the victim on high alert and makes them walk on eggshells to avoid any "mistake" that might lead to withdrawn affection. When the inevitable transgression happens, they punish their victims through stonewalling, shouting, or emotional and physical abuse.

A narcissist who does not get the special treatment he craves (his "supply" of attention, admiration, approval, etc.) cannot function. At this point, the cycle may repeat itself with a new round of love bombing to regain control of the victim. Love bombing is a tool for manipulation and control, not real love!

Surprisingly, narcissists and psychopaths are particularly drawn to successful, smart, and empathetic women, not because they are weak, but quite the opposite. I never believed I would be a target. I am smart and analytical, and I default to fact-checking—I consider myself not easily manipulated. I discovered, however, that self-centered men want to prey on a strong woman who is empathetic and has a lot to give. They need someone steady and strong—someone they can count on to be there for them while also being independent and self-sufficient, so they don't require as much care.

An empathetic woman can also tend to their childish needs and stroke their fragile egos. An overly-empathetic woman is an ideal victim because she stops empathizing with herself and starts to make excuses for him instead. I did that with my ex; now I know I can never change another man, nor should I ever make excuses for him or his behavior.

The more successful, beautiful, or strong-willed a woman is, the more the conquest will fuel a narcissist's ego. They feel special through association—a woman who will reflect well on them makes an even more attractive target.

Since they take pleasure in manipulating and destroying their victims, the higher the victim falls from a physically, mentally, socially, financially, or emotionally strong place, the higher the pleasure for the abuser. Some narcissists try to destroy others as a reflection of their own low self-esteem, while others simply take pleasure in the destruction. In either case, a narcissist's ultimate goal is to gain control over others. To do it, they will use any tactic, charm, or talent they have, including *gaslighting* (making you question what you believe is real), blaming you or others, playing the victim, attacking you, promising to change, or making you afraid ("You'll never find anyone else to love you."). In short, narcissists are not capable of change or real love; if you are dating one, get out quickly with no contact whatsoever.

The good news is that narcissists are easy to identify because they don't hide their traits. If you ask them to describe how they are better than others, or how the world would be a better place if they ruled it, it can be easy to expose them early on. It can be very hard for narcissists to accept criticism, as well, and they become angry or strike back at real or perceived judgments. They will also not take no for an answer. A narcissist might explode at refusals or denials. A healthy partner, on the other hand, will accept constructive criticism and admit when they are wrong.

One thing that I did not know before my ordeal with Don was that narcissists *are* able to empathize. On a few occasions, I could tell Don was sensitive to how I was feeling—when my mood or tone of voice changed, for example. Now I know that some narcissists can actually feel what the other person feels, but cannot imagine the impact of their behavior on others. Some narcissists don't want to hurt other people but are so into themselves that they either don't realize when they do, or they don't care.

If you're stuck with a narcissist, sociopath, borderline, or other personality, end the relationship immediately. Delete and block their number and all social media connections. Allow no contact *whatsoever*. They are not capable of changing. They only see people as tools to exploit and are incapable of love. They are never sorry, and will never feel guilt or remorse. Don never apologized about lying to me or trying to hurt me—the final proof that he was a narcissist. My friend later jokingly said, "An apology from him would be nice, but we are not delusional."

Narcissists and sociopaths don't have true confidence and high self-esteem within. They rely on other people to supply it, like oxygen. When you cut their "supply" by breaking up with them, they will want to keep you—you must be clear and disconnect completely. When they see that they have nothing to gain from you and cannot manipulate or control you any longer, you may be fortunate enough to never hear from them again—they just move to their next victim. I suspect Don will never contact me again because he knows he has nothing to gain.

Another thing I didn't know at the time is that narcissists' biggest fear is to feel humiliated or inferior. When I broke up with Don and exposed his web of lies and narcissistic behavior, he denied it (of course), but it was clear that he felt humiliated and inferior. He could not come up with any excuse or manipulation or any more lies that I would ever believe. His self-esteem was completely shot—I believe that is one of the reasons he simply sat outside in his car for over an hour, unable to move. Perhaps it was the first time he was exposed so soon—whatever the case, I'm glad he's not my problem.

Ironically, I ultimately took advantage of him. It was unintentional, of course, but I enjoyed being pursued, the fun, how he adored me, the play, the romance, the intimacy, the sex, the amazing experiences we had together (which he paid for!), the sweetness and kindness—all without suffering any of the ugliness that would have surely come later.

I did not enjoy being lied to and manipulated, but in retrospect, there were a few more warning signs I ignored. Ultimately, I learned a valuable lesson for the future. The break-up empowered me tremendously, and I am at peace.

The point is to continuously check whether you have a healthy

relationship with good boundaries or whether you have any problems such as control issues. If they are taking it too fast, for example,
and you ask them to slow down, a manipulator will continue to
push you to move forward, while someone who respects you will
slow down. Real love takes time to develop and is patient, kind,
gentle, and respectful. If you draw a boundary, a decent person will
respect it.

If you feel like your partner has control issues, confront them.
If they do not pull back or respect your wishes, then you have an
issue. You may not have a narcissist or psychopath on your hands,
but it has to be addressed early on for the relationship. If it can't
be dealt with, break up and move on. Trust your intuition. If your
relationship is moving too fast for you or seems too good to be true,
it probably is.

Screening is Your First Defense

There are a near-infinite number of reasons for why relationships
fail, including trust issues, different expectations, compatibility
issues, differences in priorities, lack of respect, emotional or physical abuse, power struggles, and many more.

You can't see the future or read minds, but I truly believe my
system and the tools in this book will weed out most or all of those
issues early on in a relationship before you are in too deep. I am not
suggesting the system is perfect, or that you will never be hurt. But
an approach to dating that focuses on being clear about your goals,
and taking the time to find compatibility instead of being seduced
by chemistry, can go a long way to fostering long term success.

Although not all of my relationships worked, and many of them
ended in break-ups, I was never emotionally devastated when they

did. It was never long before I was back to swiping again because I knew that the problem was with the match, not some fundamental problem with me. Being clear and following a process not only helps find better matches, but it helps to deal with mismatches, too.

The Four Horsemen

Dr. John Gottman is an author and brilliant psychologist who focuses on relationships. His research, called "The Four Horsemen of the Apocalypse," can predict with fair certainty when a romantic relationship will end.

In his work, Gottman identified four behaviors that predict relationship failure: *criticism, defensiveness, contempt,* and *stonewalling.* Couples in healthy relationships do not engage in any of these behaviors. When a relationship is troubled, however, these behaviors begin to surface and foreshadow the end.

They certainly predicted the end of mine. After years of criticism and defensiveness from my ex, I developed contempt for him that eventually ended the relationship for me.

According to Dr. Gottman, men are much more likely to stonewall than women (up to 85% of men versus 15% women), and they will withdraw emotionally from conflict discussions while women remain emotionally engaged. Another interesting point Dr. Gottman's research discovered is that when a woman stonewalls, it is predictive of divorce.

One of my ex-boyfriends had an anger issue that would leave him trapped in his own head. He was, and still is, a wonderful man—he's independent, honest, empathetic, and supportive. I knew something was wrong, however, because he did not call me or text me for a few days—a vast difference from the usual multiple texts and daily calls. I kept asking him what was wrong and if everything was okay, but he did not respond to texts or calls for over a week.

I really thought the relationship was over, and I texted him to ask if he wanted to break up. He immediately called back and said he did not want to break up, but that he was really angry with me. I said his behavior was childish, and we needed to be able to talk the situation through and resolve it. I had no clue what I did to make him angry, but I respected his right to feel that way. Still, if he couldn't engage and discuss things as an adult, I couldn't build a long-term relationship with him.

He did not offer an explanation and remained stuck in his anger without asking for my point of view or perspective on why I acted the way I did. He was punishing me for something I did not know I did. Had he said, "I am mad at you because of *x*, I just need a break for a day or a few days. I'll contact you when I am less angry so we can talk," it would have been okay. Even breaking up with a reason would have been better than the silent treatment.

I was especially sensitive to this because it was one of the go-to tools in my ex-husband's passive-aggressive arsenal. Eventually, I developed resilience to it because I became apathetic towards him. Instead of feeling contempt, which would also hurt me, I ended up becoming indifferent and not caring at all about him. What he does no longer affects me emotionally, but this type of behavior from a partner is unacceptable.

After fully discussing the situation with my boyfriend, I gave him a second chance on the condition that the behavior would not be repeated. Sadly, a few months later, the red line was crossed again. He was angry at me for another issue and ignored me for a week. I decided to end the relationship because of it. He did not want to break up, but I no longer allow my red lines to be crossed. I forgave him the first time because he was unaware, but there were no second chances.

He was heartbroken, and so was I. He did not make it easy on me and came to see me after; he hugged and kissed me, and said that he missed me and wanted me back. A few days later, he texted me: *Just thought of you! I am alone in the crowd. Wish you were here.*

It was difficult, but ending it was the right thing to do.

* * *

If I had a magic wand, I'd like a chance to break up with my partners at the *beginning* of a relationship so I could get a preview of how psychotic they can be when the relationship ends. It might be better if all relationships started with a gory break-up so you can experience for yourself your partner's worst behaviors upfront. Then, if you're up for the ride, get back together, and build a relationship!

I'm joking, of course, but it's worth remembering that red flags early on are not to be taken lightly—they can be signs of more difficult things to come.

CHAPTER 15

Compatibility Tools

What counts in making a happy marriage is not so much how compatible you are but how you deal with incompatibility.

-Leo Tolstoy

By now, I hope you're making progress, with at least a few first dates under your belt, some candidates screened out, and perhaps some second or further dates with others. Perhaps you're even ready to become exclusive! Regardless of where you are in your journey, remember that it's best to strive for progress, not perfection.

In this chapter, I want to give you what I call "compatibility tools" that you can use to further analyze the characteristics, personality, and communication style of a potential long-term partner. Not everyone will need or use these deeper-level screening tools, but I've found them very useful for efficiently screening and disqualifying suitors.

These compatibility tools will be most beneficial after the first date, which is more superficial and meant to determine if you like the other person and if there is potential for chemistry for both of you.

On the second date and beyond, however, these tools can help you not only find compatibility but uncover the lies, games, and dishonesty that, unfortunately, are not uncommon in dating. Using them will help you get to the truth faster and find compatibility sooner.

Big Five / OCEAN Model

The "Big Five" personality traits (also known as the five-factor or OCEAN model) is a collection of personality traits that we all share. Any person can be rated on a spectrum for each trait, and each individual's place on the spectrum is determined by a balanced combination of nature (the person's genes) and nurture (how their overall environment shaped them).

The five (OCEAN) factors are:

1. Openness to Experiences

This defines whether a person is inventive and curious at one end of the spectrum, versus consistent and cautious at the other. You are more open to experiences if you are more creative, have an appreciation for art, emotions, adventure, imagination, unusual ideas, and curiosity. You are willing to try new things and are generally aware of your feelings. People with low openness, on the other hand, seek to gain fulfillment through perseverance and are more pragmatic and data-driven. Those with extremely low openness can be dogmatic and closed-minded. Those at the other extreme can be flighty and irresponsible.

2. Conscientiousness

This factor assesses whether a person is efficient and organized at one end of the spectrum versus easy-going and careless at the other. Conscientious people are self-disciplined, focused, and strive for achievement. They like to plan, pay attention to details, and like order and schedules, but at the extreme, they can be stubborn and rigid. Low conscientiousness is associated with flexibility and spontaneity, but also forgetfulness, and in the extreme can be unreliable and sloppy.

3. Extroversion

This spectrum spans from outgoing and energetic on one side to solitary and reserved on the other. Extroverts are full of energy and thrive on engaging with the external world, including socializing and engaging in activities with others. They are enthusiastic, action-oriented individuals. They are assertive, talkative, and enjoy social interactions. Conversely, introverts engage less socially and are more reserved in social situations. Their energy levels are lower, and they are quiet and low-key. They need less stimulation and need more time alone to recharge, preferring to quietly read a book rather than go to a party.

4.Agreeableness

This factor is a determination of whether a person is friendly and compassionate at one end of the spectrum versus challenging and detached at the other. Agreeableness is a general concern for social harmony and getting along with others. Agreeable people are generally optimistic, considerate, kind, generous, trusting (and trustworthy), helpful, and willing to compromise with others. Disagreeable people generally place their self-interest first, which can make them unapologetically dogged, and help them advance their goals in life and get their way. On the other hand, they are prone to not care about the well-being of others and be suspicious, unfriendly, uncooperative, challenging, argumentative, or untrustworthy.

5. Neuroticism

The fifth of the Big Five personality traits describes whether a person is sensitive and nervous at one end of the spectrum versus secure and confident at the other. Neurotic people are generally more stressed, pessimistic, and experience more negative emotions. They are more often in a bad mood, and in extreme cases, can be emotionally unstable, making it more difficult for them to make decisions and think clearly. People who score low in neuroticism are more optimistic, are not easily upset, and are more emotionally stable overall. They are calmer, rarely feel sad, and can usually cope effectively with stress.

Take a few minutes to reflect on where you are on each of the spectrums. Where are your best friends or other important relationships? Where do your worst relationships fall?

I was in a relationship with someone who was very disagreeable and neurotic. One of his favorite pastimes was to insult and criticize other people, and he generally lacked concern for and interest in others. (A category that often included me). He was also easily upset and worried about the smallest of things. Those traits were difficult for me and dragged me down. I want and now *require* a partner who is more agreeable and relaxed most of the time.

DISC Profile

DISC is an acronym for Dominant, Influential, Steady, and Compliant. It's a profiling tool I use to evaluate whether someone is a possible match.

The DISC profile is an assessment of communication styles, and it is relatively easy to use. If you've had much sales or business training, you may have used DISC before. Here's how the four styles relate to romantic relationships.

1.Dominant

As the name suggests, this is a person who takes charge, who is a leader by nature. *Dominant* people are generally interested in the big picture and bottom line, and not the finer details. Do not waste time describing to them the minute details, advantages and disadvantages, or anything superfluous; they will quickly cut you off. These "Type-As" or "Alphas" are also bold risk-takers who are easily bored. Many executives and managers are highly dominant, and this certainly carries over into relationships.

Dominant personalities like to control or win over other people, which can be problematic for relationships. Beware of extremes in this category, specifically control freaks. If you're dominant, even if you are right and you "win," you'll often hurt the relationship, especially if the topic is inconsequential.

Dominant personalities like to assume the role of pursuer. In relationships, this is typically a male role. As discussed in prior chapters, if a woman pursues a man more than he pursues her, it can be a turn-off.

Dominant personalities often set the tone and rules in relationships, dictating what is and is not acceptable, where to go, and what to do. They will be very assertive, say what is on their mind, and directly ask for what they want. If you are not assertive enough, dominants can walk all over you. They will probably book the vacation for you—less because they want to be nice, and more because they would only stay at *that* resort, and they would only fly with *that* airline and eat *that* type of food. This is an extreme example, but it illustrates the point. Although it's not my predominant style, I have highly dominant characteristics—I would not match well with a highly dominant person. It's yet another reason to be yourself; when character traits collide, relationships tend to struggle. Better to find out sooner rather than later.

If you are a dominant person and want to improve your chances of relationship success, I recommend that you negotiate when faced with relatively insignificant conflict—practice finding compromise, especially with things that matter less to you. I am not extremely picky about restaurants, for example, so I almost always let my date choose. Participate jointly in decision-making and make requests instead of issuing demands. Ask directly for your partner's view, and validate and respect it even when it differs from yours.

If you are dating a dominant person and feel that they exercise too much control, I recommend you talk to them directly about the behavior and how it makes you feel. For example: *It bothered me when you demanded that I change my plans for Friday night in order to meet you, instead of following through on our Thursday plans. It made me feel unimportant and that you view my time as less valuable than yours.*

Stick to the facts and how it made you feel, and make a suggestion for them on how to improve for next time: *Maybe next time, you could ask me ahead of time and let me choose the night and the place.*

You may need to spell out for them that you want to be a part of the decision-making and negotiate with them to reach common ground. If they cannot live with that, and you cannot either, *cut 'em loose!*

2. Influential

The *influential* personality is a socially extroverted person who is all about people—the extreme "E" in the previous OCEAN model. They want to get to know you and are generally charming and charismatic. Most influentials know they can best sway others with honey rather than vinegar. Their "honey" is to smile, be sociable and gregarious, and have a real interest in others.

Influentials are the social butterflies, the life of the party. They like to "hold court" and be noticed and admired. The upside to this in a relationship is that they seek the approval of others—they like to please people, including their significant other.

Influential people also love to have fun. They like excitement and variety, romance, and they enjoy the chase in dating. One potential downside to dating an influential is that they will often want to date multiple people simultaneously until they are absolutely sure about you. That can sometimes take more time than you're willing to give.

Influential is my dominant style. If I were planning a vacation, I'd organize the entire thing and then excitedly tell my partner about it. I would love the romance of both the idea and trying to please my partner. But not every type appreciates that. If you are an influential, too, remember to reign in your spontaneity, particularly in planning. If you are dating a *steady* or *compliant* person (see below), let them participate in the plan-making. If your partner is more introverted, understand their need to recharge—they'll need some quiet time alone.

Take pride and rejoice in small changes that push the relationship forward instead of waiting for that huge win. And when you are fairly certain that a partner is for you, commit to them wholeheartedly, instead of feeling confined by the relationship and wanting to date multiple people.

If you are the one dating an influential person, pay extra attention to your partner, and display your affection and admiration both privately and publicly. Plan and share fun activities. Bring excitement, romance, and surprises to your dating life—laughter and surprises energize influentials. Try to avoid dull, routine, and predictable dates, like going to the same restaurants over and over or doing similar activities.

Many influentials have a strong need for independence. They want to be able to maintain relationships outside of dating. Be prepared to give them space if they need it.

3. Steady

A *steady* personality is oriented toward people and relationships, but unlike an influential, a steady wants more cooperation, consensus, support, and understanding. A steady person will want to accommodate their partner, ask their opinion, and get their input on big decisions. (Unlike an influential, a steady will have a challenging time making big decisions.)

While a steady person likes to give and receive attention and affection, they usually prefer a one-on-one connection over socializing with dozens of people.

Most steady people are risk-averse—routine, familiarity, and comfort are essential. As a result, they tend to stay in a relationship long after it's no longer beneficial. Approval of others is very important to a steady person, and many will do just about anything to please their partner if it helps maintain peace and the status quo.

In contrast with an influential, before booking (or even beginning to plan) a vacation, a steady will ask their partner where they would like to go and stay, what they would like to eat, what activities they want to do, all in an effort to accommodate their partner. A steady will be hesitant, even if asked directly, to say something like, "Well, since you asked, I really would prefer to go to the beach instead of New York City."

If you are the steady one in a relationship, be sure to know what your boundaries are and communicate them to your partner. Remember that you *can* say *no*. In fact, you really should say it more often—learn to voice your opinions and thoughts, be assertive, and stand your ground. Otherwise, your partner can walk all over you.

While you may genuinely find delight in pleasing your partner (and there is nothing wrong with that!), you first need to know how to please yourself. Pay attention to your thoughts and feelings—otherwise, you run the risk of creating a monster in your partner who has become accustomed to always getting their way. Once that expectation is established, it can be difficult to fix without conflict.

If you are dating a steady person, use a slower pace to advance the relationship, especially at first. Try not to do anything unexpected; instead, let them know what to expect and have a routine in place that they can get used to.

To help them venture out of their comfort zone, surprise them in small ways. Try a piece of pie from their favorite restaurant rather than a two-week trip to Europe. Be steady, calm, and predictable, and ask for their opinion and consent in advance if you need to change something.

Encourage them to share their thoughts and feelings and to be more assertive. Support and validate them when you disagree, and as with any relationship, do not let disagreements escalate into arguments if possible.

With a steady partner, share things that are going on in your life, including your interests and friends. Offer sincere admiration and attention, steadily pursue them, and slowly progress to each new level of the relationship.

4. Compliant

A *compliant* person is all about facts, details, data, and information. They want more nitty-gritty, less big picture. Compliant people seek acknowledgment from their partners. They desire to know that they are right (as opposed to *having* to be right), and they focus on the facts.

As a result, they look more objectively at potential partners and can analyze their advantages and disadvantages—even using pros and cons lists and spreadsheets. They also prefer to date only one person at a time.

Compliants are rational and cautious and are not likely to be swept off their feet. Rather, they prefer to spend quality time with a potential partner and evaluate them carefully over time. Only after they are fairly certain will they allow themselves to fall in love.

Like dominants, compliants need to be right, but rather than shoving it down their partner's throat, they need the reassurance that they are. This sometimes trumps the feelings of their partner, and the relationship may suffer. As with a dominant, if you argue about something small, even if you are right, it can damage the relationship. You may have won the argument, but you can lose in the long term by hurting your partner.

Using the same vacation-planning scenario, if you are booking a vacation for a compliant partner, you'd best show them all the facts beforehand, and explain why you chose the specific destination, the specific hotel, etc. Furthermore, make sure you have compared offerings, gotten the best deal, and are within budget. Better yet, if you can relinquish control of these types of decisions, you may want to just let the compliant partner take care of everything!

Compliant people are generally slower in speech. They're also slow to make a decision, but unlike a steady personality, they don't need consensus. Accuracy and precision are very important to compliant people, as is staying within the rules. If you want to impress a compliant person, focus on details, facts, data points, and, if possible, show them charts or graphs or numbers. You'll need them to support your case.

Finally, most compliant people are introverts. They need to maintain their independence and have some alone time to recharge.

If you are a compliant person, allow yourself to open up to new experiences at times, and appreciate the effort and the pleasant surprises of a partner who is trying to delight you. Offer sincere compliments, and learn how to accept and appreciate when your partner does the same.

Try to open up emotionally. Talk about yourself and your feelings and have the courage to be vulnerable. Participate more in the relationship, and as it progresses, take less time alone. Try to curb your need to be right; many things are far too small and inconsequential to argue about. Even if you're right about the benefits of booking your vacation on Orbitz versus Expedia, let it go. It may not be worth winning the argument if you damage the relationship.

If you are dating a compliant person, offer them exclusivity in dating as early as possible—it will be important to them. Share experiences as a couple, but try to avoid surprises or unexpected situations. Plan quality dates and deep, meaningful experiences. Act in a loving way that proves to them that you care. Tell them about yourself and share stories and opinions to help them collect enough data to evaluate you. Encourage them to open up as well, and to share their thoughts and be vulnerable. Help them to verbalize their feelings instead of engaging in only black-and-white, rational thinking. Finally, give them time alone to recharge.

Everyone has aspects of all four DISC personality styles, but typically one or two of them are most prominent. The people I know who are most successful in relationships are highly adaptable to a quality partner and can determine what behaviors they need to engage in and what behaviors they need to change to be a better partner themselves.

The goal of DISC is not to box yourself into a particular style, but rather to help you gain a more in-depth understanding of each of your preferences. I encourage you to get out of your comfort zone—stretch yourself to grow in the direction of your partner so that the relationship can flourish.

For additional information and resources on the DISC profile, go to https://www.discprofile.com.

Myers-Briggs

The Myers-Briggs Type Indicator (MBTI) is a tool that will be familiar to most people who work in corporate America. You don't need to know your type to date effectively, but some people list their Myers-Briggs personality on their profile. I use it in my work to communicate better with my team and to recruit more effectively. In dating, understanding the MBTI has helped me disqualify people quickly, or indicate an enthusiastic "thumbs up" to continue further.

There are several free MBTI assessments that both you and your potential partner can take to learn more about the sixteen main personality types. I've used it as a way to gain insight into who I am and how I show up in a relationship, and also to understand my advantages, my less desirable traits, and who I am most likely to be compatible with.

If you don't know your personality type, I highly recommend the experience. Knowing yourself and your communication style offers value in all areas of life, not just dating. You can even learn which celebrities share your traits! The more you know about yourself and the more informed you are, the more selective you can be, and the more likely you are to choose a good mate.

When both people know their type, it's easier to know if the two of you will be compatible. I have even been so bold as to ask someone to complete the MBTI prior to a second date! It can certainly be used after you have met and found some chemistry, but stating it upfront on your profile can make screening easier. You can discover your profile at www.16personalities.com.

* * *

You certainly don't need to use all of these tools in your quest for compatibility. But they are established, respected, and tried and true. They can't *hurt* and might help you better understand and communicate with your partner. Even without a partner, you'll learn more about yourself.

Take some time to learn who you are. If you find a tool that resonates with you, consider using it as a screening tool or as a way of improving a budding relationship. You'll find your way to compatibility faster and might discover something about yourself that will pay dividends for a lifetime. If nothing else, compatibility tools make for great conversation!

CHAPTER 16

Romance Tools

Love is that condition in which the happiness of another person is essential to your own.

-Robert Heinlein

In the last chapter, we looked at tools that can help you identify compatibility in potential partners. By looking at traits and behaviors through different lenses, you can get a clearer picture of not only someone else's character but also your own.

Once you identify compatibility, there are specific tools you can use to enhance a relationship with a quality person. Think of it as the next step on your journey, one focused not so much on elimination, but on growing what you've found.

Body Language

The most important tool in your arsenal is your ability to read body language. There is no substitute for understanding nonverbal communication, and you can only effectively do it in person on a real date.

246 | Karen Weinstock

Because many people do not bring their authentic selves to dating and relationships and may mislead, lie, or play games, body language offers us a shortcut in getting to the truth, offering a glimpse of a person's inner feelings, thoughts, and intentions.

The words we speak carry far less of our meaning than you might imagine. Nonverbal communication makes up over 65% of the communication between people—between romantic partners, it can approach 100%. When you are in sync with a partner, even receiving a simple look or touch can be enough to let you know exactly how they feel.

Women are generally better than men at deciphering non-verbal communication. (We're usually better at communicating than men, period.) But dating presents a challenge. On first and second dates, in particular, you are often excited, distracted by the tricks of chemistry. That can make analyzing body language difficult. In addition, because you both presumably want to make a good first impression, and you don't know each other well, it's difficult to know what normal or "baseline" behavior is. While it's relatively easy to notice if your close family members or friends behave differently because you've been interacting with them for years, the task is harder with strangers.

The most significant marker of body language during a date is the face. How relaxed does the other person look? Do they smile a lot, and is the smile genuine? Do they maintain eye contact? If they do not, it can be a sign that they are not that interested, that they disagree with you, or that they are bored.

If a date consistently looks into your eyes, particularly while the two of you are talking, it's a sign of interest. A slight nodding of the head is an indication of cooperation and agreement. If he mirrors your gestures, he is trying to get in sync with you because he likes you. However, if he rubs his face, he may feel emotional discomfort.

Over the years, I've interviewed many people and attended many networking and social functions. Those experiences gave me a head start on understanding if my date's words and actions are congruent and whether certain questions or topics cause him discomfort. Pay attention to your partner's tone of voice. Is it pleasant? Bored? Aggravated? If you feel that you are not great at reading body language, I recommend learning about the subject to better evaluate potential partners.

When one or both parties lie, the chances of meaningful connection are greatly diminished. I had a date with a man who claimed to be a confident, successful professional who appreciated a smart, independent woman. Huge lie! He spent our first date with his arms closed off, neurotically looking at the table or behind his shoulder, fidgeting nervously.

I noticed his body language and was taken aback. After the date was over, he texted me. *Thank you for the wonderful date, I had a great time with you.*

I pressed him about his behavior. *It did not look to me like you were having such a good time.* He replied, *Honestly, I was incredibly nervous. Aside from being incredibly attractive, you are so accomplished and traveled. I was very intimidated. Could I have another chance over dinner?*

My answer was a polite no. If he felt intimidated and insecure on the first date, we'd never work long-term. The date was a waste of my time (and money since I had to pay a babysitter).

If both parties are truthful, there is a much better chance to build a lasting and meaningful relationship. Honesty and vulnerability promote trust and bonding. You do not need to be liked by every person you date, but you do need to be *honest* with them.

Authenticity and Vulnerability

A consistent theme in this book is that throughout the dating process, you must be authentic. The only way a relationship will work is for both you and your partner to be completely yourself. After all, why would you want to be with someone who does not like the real *you*?

Dr. Brené Brown, a vulnerability expert, encourages us to have the courage to show up and play full out even when we can't know the outcome. Be emotionally exposed. Get comfortable facing uncertainty and taking emotional risks even though you will fail, and at times, be hurt.

Emotional openness, vulnerability, and exchange of intimate thoughts and feelings build trust with your partner. Trust is something that you build over time, but it begins when you have the courage to share with your partner. Cultivate your own authenticity and let go of what other people think.

In every interaction with your partner, especially when they share something vulnerable with you, choose to go towards your partner instead of away from them. When you go toward your partner with love, empathy, and compassion, the relationship will grow. Relationships begin to die when your partner stops caring or paying attention to you.

Be Considerate

While you do need to think of yourself, you also have to remember your partner's needs. One of the most important things in a relationship is to be considerate. Figure out what makes them tick, what delights them and why, and just do it! If you can act with dignity toward your partner and keep their best interest at heart, you have a good chance of making it work.

If my partner learns how to dance salsa with me, for example, it would be a huge gift—even if he has two left feet and prefers to stay home and watch Netflix! His consideration is what matters.

Likewise, when he understands that spending time apart and engaging in separate activities makes us miss each other, that too is considerate. Be thoughtful and flexible—your partner will thank you.

Five To One Ratio

According to researcher Dr. John Gottman, there is a healthy "recipe" for successful relationships—a magic ratio of five positive interactions to one negative interaction between partners.

The reason for the high ratio is that negative interactions between couples are so devastating and taken so personally that both parties need to invest more in return to compensate. Stable and happy couples share many more positive feelings and interactions than negative ones—things like warm looks, smiles, physical touches, hugs, kisses, compliments, active listening, and appreciation.

Daily criticism and ignoring were my ex's weapons of choice. If someone is engaging in these negative behaviors, especially early on in the relationship, get out and get out fast!

Don't keep score, but keep the ratio in mind.

Discuss Issues Openly

If there is an issue, no matter how small or insignificant it may seem, talk about it openly. Communicate with the intention of understanding where the other person is coming from. What is their viewpoint, and why did they do what they did? Seek first to understand then be understood.

Do you have the need to always be right? You may be paying a high price. Even though you may be right, you may be killing the relationship. The need to be right all the time suggests you lack empathy toward your partner and are not trying to see things from their point of view. As the saying goes, *you can be right, or you can be happy.*

You can only build a dream relationship by being completely honest with each other about things that bother you. If both parties are genuinely interested in building a relationship, they will change their behavior to accommodate and please their partner. If they do not change their behavior despite multiple requests, they are either not capable of changing, or not interested.

If you discuss issues openly and truly understand each other better, you will avoid misunderstandings and resentment. Even though it may be uncomfortable in the short term to discuss difficult problems, honesty and transparency always win in the long term. And, if someone is not able to discuss difficult issues and truly listen and work to resolve them, are they *really* well-matched with you?

Handling Disagreements

When issues do surface, how do you communicate them with your partner? The best way is to express how you feel about your partner or behavior they engaged in, without blaming, name-calling, or anything similarly off-putting. For example: "*I felt angry when you were 15 minutes late for dinner without letting me know you'll be late.*" It's an effective way because your partner cannot argue with how you feel.

I learned a valuable technique in therapy called Imago, which comprises three steps: mirroring, validating, and empathizing. First, *mirror* the other person by effectively repeating what your partner said. Mirroring helps the other person feel heard. You can also invite your partner to tell you more.

After mirroring, comes *validating*, in which the person listening tells the person speaking that what they said makes sense to them and gives them a reason why. This step helps the other person feel understood and reassures them that they are not crazy.

In the last step, which is *empathizing*, the person listening identifies what feeling(s) the other person has. For example: "*You probably feel angry, disappointed, and unimportant that I didn't let you know I would be an hour late for dinner.*"

You can take turns sending and receiving messages with your partner, mirroring and validating if you both have unresolved issues to discuss.

See the Best

Researchers discovered that the most common quality in couples who lasted the longest was the ability for each partner to see and assume the best in the other.

If a partner is late for dinner, for example, my default thought isn't *he is cheating on me* or *he doesn't care about me*. Instead, seeing the best would lead me to think *he's probably stuck at an important meeting and will call or come home as soon as he can.*

When both partners assume the best in each other, they also bring out the best in each other!

Love Languages

An invaluable process while growing a relationship is set out in the book *The Five Love Languages: How to Express Heartfelt Commitment to Your Mate* by Gary Chapman. In it, Dr. Chapman describes five predominant ways that romantic partners express and experience love. If you and your partner don't share the same love language, you can learn to "speak" your partner's love language, and they can learn to speak yours.

Here are the five love languages, with a discussion of their impact on relationships.

1. Receiving Gifts

If receiving gifts is your primary love language, then you love the thoughtfulness and effort behind a gift and see it as proof that you are cared for and appreciated. For you, gifts are the physical representation of love, and you treasure them. If your partner brings you a thoughtless gift or forgets a gift on your birthday or anniversary, you feel devastated. Similarly, *you* will tend to express your love for your partner by giving them gifts on special occasions or "just because."

2. Quality Time

If quality time is your primary love language, you'll want your partner's full and undivided attention. Quality time means sharing quality experiences, activities, and conversations—without phones, TV, or other distractions.

You feel truly loved by your partner when they value time with you and make it a priority. If this is the love language you primarily speak, you will tend to seek one-on-one time with your mate. You're much more likely to plan a trip for just the two of you than to give your partner material things.

3. Words of Affirmation

If words of affirmation are your primary love language, you feel that words speak louder than actions. You want your partner to shower you with compliments, but you also need them to be genuine and heartfelt. You want more than "I love you" or "You are beautiful" (although those are important). You also want to hear what makes you special, why your partner loves and respects you, and why they find you attractive. You appreciate encouragement, support, and kind affirmations; conversely, insults or criticisms are especially hurtful.

4. Physical Touch

If physical touch is your primary love language, you want to literally *feel* loved by your partner, not only through sex (which will be very important), but also through kisses, holding hands, hugs, cuddling, massage, or any intentional touch from your partner that shows they are excited to be with you. Physical distance is very difficult for you. And touch goes both ways—you will want to touch *and* be touched.

5. Acts of Service

If your primary love language is acts of service, you feel most loved by your partner when they do things for you just because or to help you or alleviate your responsibilities. You value when your partner does the laundry, cooks for you, lets you sleep in, takes care of the kids, or washes your car. Those actions are what make you feel loved, and it will probably be your tendency to express love back the same way.

A side note on acts of service: According to many women *and* scientific research, men who share more in household responsibilities (cleaning, laundry, cooking, etc.) generally have happier marriages, more satisfied partners, and better sex life! This applies *regardless* of which love language the woman prefers. Ladies, if you ask him nicely to do these things for you and show your appreciation, it will also enhance his feelings of manliness.

Likewise, regardless of a man's love language, sexual satisfaction will generally make him a kinder, more loving partner, and result in a happier relationship.

While everyone appreciates all five love languages to some degree, most people have a clear preference for one or two. Chapman's theory is that each person has one primary and one secondary love language and that most people express love to their partners in their own language by default. They mean well, tending to give in the language they prefer to receive. But the most successful relationships are created when each partner expresses love in the *other's* primary love language(s).

I have a girlfriend, Lori, who was married for twenty years to a quality man, Chad. He was good-looking, loyal, kind, had a great job, and was a wonderful dad. On paper, they were the perfect couple, and Lori was the envy of many of her friends and co-workers.

For twenty years without fail, Chad never missed an opportunity to send Lori flowers on every birthday, anniversary, and Valentine's Day, and at other spontaneous times just to tell her he loved her! He bought extremely thoughtful gifts and talked openly about how much he loved her, how beautiful and smart she was, and what he appreciated about her.

But Lori craved two things from Chad: one, that he spend more time with her, and two, physical affection and sex. She wanted him to get up on Saturday mornings and go to the farmers market with her. She wanted them to travel together and take romantic trips without the kids. She wanted the physical and emotional intimacy of an active sex life, including frequent hugs and kisses, and public displays of affection. She wanted him to sit outside with her while she planted flowers, even if he was just drinking a beer and they were listening to music and laughing. It didn't matter if he helped her, just that he was *close* to her. Then she wanted him to drag her inside the house and ravish her, even if she was sweaty and covered in dirt.

Chad and Lori ended up in two different stints of counseling. She often felt guilty that she wanted more from him when he was otherwise so incredibly and genuinely *good* to her. Lori begged him not to go back to school to get an advanced degree—even though it would mean more household income, it would also mean more time away from her. And she was ashamed to ever share with her girlfriends that her lack of a good sex life with her husband was so important to her, imagining them rolling their eyes, saying, "Cry me a river!"

These two people, who were otherwise quite compatible, who rarely fought, and who seemed to be the perfect couple, ultimately divorced after a twenty-year marriage. They broke each other's hearts as well as their children's, all because they didn't understand love languages. It was as if he was telling her all day that he loved her, but in his native tongue of German, and she was telling him all day that she loved him, but in her native tongue of French. No matter how much they truly loved each other, that language barrier eventually killed their relationship because they never learned to speak each other's language and understand and appreciate how much their partner really loved them.

Don't make the same mistake as Chad and Lori. Discover what your love language is, and that of a potential partner. The book is a great read, and you can take the love language test at www.5love-languages.com.

Attachment Styles

Another vital tool to grow a budding relationship is described in the book *Attached* by Amir Levine and Rachel Heller. In it, the authors outline three main *attachment styles*—how people perceive and respond to intimacy in romantic relationships. About 50% of people are *secure*, 25% are *avoidant*, 20% are *anxious*, and the remaining 5% are a combination of two styles, *anxious-avoidant.*

Reading this book helped me understand my own attachment style (secure), and also how to quickly determine the attachment style of my partner. It's an excellent book and worth adding to your toolkit.

Here is a summary of the three main attachment styles and how they apply to dating.

1. Secure

Secure people are warm, affectionate, loving, and feel, well, *secure,* and comfortable with intimacy. They clearly communicate their wishes and needs, and are open about what they like and do not like in both a relationship and a partner. They can enjoy being intimate without becoming overly worried about the relationship and can read their partner's emotional cues so they can be there for them when needed.

2. Anxious

Anxious people crave intimacy and depend on a partner to provide it. They are highly preoccupied with the relationship, which takes a lot of their energy because they constantly want to be closer to their partners. It's very difficult for them when a partner does not seem to reciprocate, and this can make them very insecure. Those with an anxious attachment style are often overly sensitive to small changes in their partner's behavior and take things too personally. They are upset easily and may say things they later regret.

An anxious person's biggest fear is that if they do something wrong, their partner will leave them. As a result, they cling to their partner for dear life, sometimes "walking on eggshells" and not communicating their own needs for fear of losing the relationship.

3. Avoidant

Avoidant people do not want intimacy, because for them, it means losing their independence. They keep chasing the next relationship, unable to commit or go deeper. For avoidants, getting into a

258 | Karen Weinstock

deep, meaningful relationship is a scary prospect. Their independence and autonomy are more important than intimacy. Because they often feel uncomfortable with too much closeness, they tend to keep an emotional distance from their partners. They hate any attempt of control from the other partner.

Note that there is a higher percentage of avoidants on online apps. They tend to be serial daters who keep chasing the perfect partner (who doesn't exist), and avoiding intimacy and long-term commitments even when they find a good match. By comparison, both secure and anxious attachment-style people match fairly quickly once they find a suitable partner. They know that they can never find a perfect partner, so they never search for perfection in the first place. They realize that relationships take effort. *Secure* people will tell their partner what they do and don't like, ask their partner to make changes, and change themselves to make the relationship work. Only if the relationship does not work will they break it off and go back to dating.

A secure-avoidant and secure-anxious couple can work because the secure partner can stretch the avoidant or anxious person, and can also stretch themselves to accommodate the other's needs. The biggest trouble in relationships occurs with avoidant-anxious couples, because one person (the anxious) pursues intimacy and requires it, but the other (the avoidant) runs from it. The book *Attached* has good insights and tips on how to deal with these situations.

Since I am less likely to match well with an avoidant, I try to determine the attachment style from a man's profile. If I can't, but am otherwise interested, I will ask probing questions by text and in person—an approach that has allowed me to dodge a few unlikely matches.

As a secure person, I much prefer dating another secure person. I had an ex who was an anxious style, and his insecurities drove me crazy. He had a hard time allowing me to have fun without him, which soon conflicted with my need for independence.

* * *

Romance tools have a dual purpose. They not only help screen potential suitors at the beginning of a relationship, but they also help enhance an established relationship by allowing you to better understand each other. Love languages, attachment styles, and body language can play as important a role after twenty years of marriage as they do on a first date.

Of course, no tool is an instant solution. Evaluating compatibility takes time and works best over many different settings and scenarios. You'll want to watch how your partner behaves not only with you but with your friends, too. You'll want to see them with their children and yours, how they behave at your home and theirs, and how they behave at work or on vacation. Understanding your partner isn't one tool or one time; it's a process.

Sometimes, unfortunately, that process ends in parting ways. The next chapter will help you deal with how to break up with someone and how to deal with rejection if someone breaks up with you.

260 | K<small>AREN</small> W<small>EINSTOCK</small>

CHAPTER 17

Break-Up and Rejection

I didn't lose you. You lost me. You'll search for me inside of everyone you're with, and I won't be found.

-R.H. Sin

You've had your first date, and it was *dreamy.*

You felt immediate chemistry and perhaps had several more dates. You had great sex repeatedly and even spent a weekend away together. You see huge potential for a long-term relationship based on the compatibility and romance tools.

Things may be going well, but you still have to evaluate your partner's behaviors and actions over time to solidify your feelings towards them. If a potential partner behaves inappropriately, and inconsistently with their words, does not fulfill your basic needs, or violates your boundaries or red lines, you have to end the relationship and move on. You must, in other words, *break up.*

This chapter will help you learn how to break up with someone gracefully and how to deal with rejection if someone breaks up with you, or even worse, ghosts you and vanishes as if they never existed.

Breaking Up Gracefully

When you are the one who decides to break it off, the decision may be easy (although not always). A break-up is easier when the relationship is in its early stages before a deep emotional connection has formed. It's also relatively easy when you discover that the two of you are clearly incompatible.

If the relationship is new—within a few dates—I suggest you call or at least text the other person to break up. Be respectful and say that you had a good time, but you do not see a long-term match. You can offer an honest reason, provided that reason isn't hurtful—that you do not want to raise small children, for example. For a break-up after one or two dates, it's fine to be non-specific, saying, "you just aren't my type" or "you're a good person but different than what I'm seeking." Thank them for the time you spent together, let them know you are moving on, and wish them well.

If you are breaking up after having sex or a longer-term relationship, you should do it in person. It's the respectful choice for a relationship you've both invested in. You may have loved them, and it may be difficult at the moment to deal with guilt, uncertainty, or tears, but it's the right thing to do.

Sometimes it *is* harder on the person who decided to break up because they feel guilty for hurting the other person, or they aren't sure they are making the right decision. They may not want to deal with an emotionally charged situation—seeing the other person cry, beg, or suffer. Hopefully, with the tools and insights in the book so far, you'll be better equipped to decide if you are indeed making the right choice.

Knowing that the person is not the right match may make a choice simpler, but it won't always make it *easier*. To exit gracefully,

262 | Karen Weinstock

you can mention what you like about them, what qualities attracted you to them, and what you enjoyed during your time together.

Be kind but unwavering. Thank them for the time together, wish them well, and move on.

It's Not You, It's Me

If you are the one who decided to break up, please do *not* cop out and use the "it's not you, it's me" excuse. First, it's untruthful—it is almost *always* about the other person, not you. Second, it sends a conflicting message and leaves the other person confused. They're getting the message that they've done nothing wrong and that there's nothing wrong with them or the match. If it were up to them, they might want to continue the relationship; instead, they're being dumped for what appears to be no reason at all. It's a lose-lose situation, even though many nice guys and gals think it's a decent or honorable way to break up. It isn't.

A guy I really liked broke up with me by text, canceling our next date because he realized that he couldn't see us as a couple in the long term.

If he had left it at that, it would have been fine. But he kept going: *I want you to know I think you are one in a million and absolutely incredible. I just need more time to work on myself... I would like to pause this, stay friends, and maybe something more in the future.*

While he was trying to be nice and to compliment me, it was a conflicting message. If he had really felt that way, he would have fought to keep me and to continue the relationship *while* he worked on himself. We could have taken things slower, or he could have allowed me to help him do the necessary self-work to get him there.

This kind of message sends false hope that getting back together or staying friends is a real possibility. It would have been better had he said, "I think you are one in a million and absolutely incredible, and I cannot see us going anywhere because you are too powerful for me." That wouldn't have been insulting nor hurtful to me because it's who I am; I can't change my personality, nor do I want to, to fit someone else.

People Don't Change

During a break-up, partners may cry, shout, or plead with you to change your mind. If you are the person being dumped, please do not behave this way. No matter how difficult the situation is for you and how sad, rejected, or angry you may be feeling, understand that the person dumping you is not your long-term partner and that they are clearing the way for you to find a better match in the future. Ending up alone is better than being with the wrong person.

If you are the one doing the breaking up and have already decided your partner is not the right person for you, stick with your decision no matter how much crying, begging, or pleading you encounter. The reality is that *you cannot change another person.* The only way a person can change is from within, and even then, people can only change so much. They can improve and change behaviors and habits, but they cannot change who they are. If you are looking for someone spontaneous and your partner does not leave his bedroom without his daily planner, he will not work for you long-term. Stick with your decision and move on.

264 | Karen Weinstock

Ghosting

Unfortunately, disinterested men and women do not always do the right thing. Instead of communicating clearly, they simply fade away, leaving the other person to wonder what happened.

People will even break off a longer-term relationship by text because they don't have the balls to face the heightened emotions of a face to face break-up. Worse, even though it would be better for both parties to find closure, many men and women choose to "ghost" and simply disappear from the other's life. This is a disrespectful and cowardly way to treat another person.

It's particularly hard when someone vanishes. If you find yourself on the receiving end of a ghosting, you may benefit from my ghosting "therapy," which can quickly bring closure with that person.

Close your eyes and imagine the ghoster standing across the room from you. Picture that person telling you kindly and sincerely why you are not the one for them. You can make up any reason you like—perhaps the ghoster says you are too devoted to your kids, your intelligence intimidates them, or they just wanted to screw around and realized you wouldn't jump right into bed.

The key is to make up whatever reason you feel best about, regardless of whether or not it is real. Perhaps your ghoster got a job offer in another city or had to move home to care for an ailing mother. Maybe he was arrested and is unable to call, had to undergo massive emergency surgery, or has checked into a mental hospital—choose whatever works best for *you*!

With your eyes still closed, thank him or her for the time you spent together and envision the ghoster sincerely telling you they are sorry that they can't see you again. Once you feel forgiveness, release them as a potential romantic partner and move on.

It doesn't matter what the real answer is. The point is to understand that *they* are not the one for *you* because *you* are not the one for *them*. Remember the funnel? The goal is to continue to disqualify, disqualify, disqualify. If someone disqualifies you first, it shouldn't rock your world or damage your self-esteem. It's a natural part of the process and one you should welcome; with every person who is disqualified (by you *or* them), you're one person closer to finding your dream relationship.

Rejection

There is no dating without *rejection*. You may feel deeply abandoned and upset if a long-term partner decides to break off a relationship with you, but rejection can come much earlier in the dating process as well. Whether it comes from people swiping away from you, potential partners disengaging, or the silence following a date you thought went very well, you *will* face rejection. Your job is to develop the skill to process it.

Rejection can be devastating, and feel just as hurtful as physical pain. Scientists, however, have figured out its cause. Through human history, we lived mainly in small groups or tribes. If we were ostracized or rejected by our group, it was essentially a death sentence—it was almost impossible to survive in nature on our own, without the community to hunt for us, care for our younglings, and protect us from predators.

While that ancestral need is now mostly gone, feelings of rejection and exclusion still hurt us deeply, including abandonment issues that stem from childhood. If your mother abandoned you as a child, at some level, you were afraid you would starve to death, or die without her protection. It may not have been true, but the emotion is primal, related to our fear of survival. To make matters worse, our brain doesn't distinguish between physical and emotional pain or even imaginary pain. Real or imagined, the pain hurts either way.

Rejection comes in many forms, some uglier than others. My ex-boyfriend, who is Indian, met a beautiful fitness trainer online. He was very fit and went to the gym daily, so they shared a similar interest. They initially got along very well and were attracted to each other. After their date, however, the woman seemed disinterested. When he asked her why, she said that she was a white Christian and was concerned that he was of a different race and religion.

He felt insulted but didn't let it get under his skin. She was bigoted, and they would never match. People who reject you for *who* you are should not be allowed to influence you. Look past them; one day, you will find someone a thousand times better.

Still, rejection can be difficult to handle. When you finally like someone a lot, and they don't reciprocate, it can be a difficult pill to swallow. I was absolutely smitten by a certain gentleman, who I found to be exactly the kind of person I could get along with. He was charming, shared many similar interests, and treated me like a queen. He even started learning salsa dancing because he wanted us to be more closely connected.

It all seemed like it was going so well until, out of the blue, he told me that he just wasn't feeling any attachment. Even though he liked me a lot and was very attracted to me, he just couldn't see me as a partner for the rest of his life.

While it hurt to know that the person I liked and thought was a good match potential did not feel the same way, I appreciated the candid conversation. He was sensitive but clear. Because of his honesty, we are still on good terms today. Transparency during rejection can help to soften the blow, but you may not always be fortunate enough to receive it.

The next time that someone rejects you, remember that the break-up is not as bad as it feels at that moment and that there are plenty of fish in the sea. Thank the person for allowing you to get one step closer to finding a match (by finding out who you did *not* match with), and continue dating.

You won't die from a break-up. It may feel like it, but you'll move on after your grieving period is over. Take your time to mourn the loss of the other person and the relationship, both of which are real. If the break-up is especially bad, take time to heal—don't instantly jump into the next relationship before you are ready.

Rebound relationships rarely work because you aren't yet prepared to open up for fear of being hurt again. When you *are* truly ready, move on, secure in the knowledge that they were not the right person for you.

During the first date or two, rejection is typically not personal. How can it be? The other person doesn't really know who you are. The break-up is only a superficial decision driven out of chemistry—something you can't create or control. Don't take it personally, because it *isn't*. If the break-up is after the first couple of dates, simply jump right back into dating.

Women are more likely to be deeply hurt and take rejection personally. We invest so much time and energy into being liked, and after all the effort, it can be challenging for us to accept rejection. Social acceptance is important to us, as well as being desirable, especially to other men. It is built into our DNA.

We tend to over-analyze, wondering what we may have done wrong, and questioning ourselves or our behavior. The more we ruminate, the more the train of automatic negative thoughts runs off the tracks and into the wild, making things worse than they really are.

I would like my potential partners to like me—who wouldn't? But whether they do or not is ultimately up to them. If they are not totally into me and who I am, they aren't the right match for me anyway—why should I care about whether they like me or not? Even if I like a man, but he doesn't reciprocate, it simply means there is no long-term potential. It is not worth the time and energy it takes to rehash every facet of the experience.

As discussed previously, resist the temptation to overthink the *why* of a break-up. There are innumerable reasons for rejection—if you can learn something, do so, but don't waste your time obsessing over *why*.

It can be much more difficult to deal with a break-up after having sex. The level of intimacy is much higher, and many women develop a strong emotional attachment. Men, however, can more often separate emotions from sexual attraction. Even if the sex is great, men don't tend to become emotionally attached.

I've worked to develop the skill of separating my emotional attachment from a man until I'm sure he is fully into me and the right match. This requires that I watch and analyze his behaviors over time. I have to have a mental and emotional connection and chemistry with the man to have sex with him in the first place, but I don't let myself fall madly in love with the man (even if the sex is great) until I know the man is truly attached and is falling in love with *me*.

It can, however, be devastating to be dumped after an attachment is formed—especially after you have fallen deeply in love. Yet, the same principals still apply. The relationship did not work, for whatever reason. While it would be good to know the *why*, it's not necessary. Even if you ask your partner why they broke up with you, they may not know the truth, or may not tell you because they don't want to hurt your feelings. Sometimes there can be great love and connection, but the timing is wrong for reasons that have nothing to do with you.

Being dumped isn't easy. You are likely to feel rejection, abandonment, and anxiety. But rest assured, you are not going to die. You will be sad. It will be difficult, perhaps for a while. But in the end, you'll be okay and will find a partner better suited to you.

Sometimes, an ex resurfaces; they may miss you and regret the break-up. That, however, is not in your control. Respect their decision to break up. Do not contact them. Don't text, call, or stalk. Leave them alone and spend the energy on healing yourself, improving yourself, having fun, and letting them miss *you*. Maintain your self-worth and dignity, and grieve the loss of your partner and your relationship.

If they love you and miss you, and you didn't go crazy at the end of the relationship, they may be back for you within thirty to sixty days. But do not contact them. I wouldn't want a man back who was foolish enough to let me go, but that's an individual decision for you to make. If the relationship was good, you are still in love, and you want to give it another shot, the choice is yours.

If you must, you can send a text seeking your partner's advice or help on something they are an "expert" on (*not* a text about getting back together), and then wait until you hear back. If you don't, or they just send back a short response, they are not interested in getting back together and never will be. It's not the relationship you were meant to have, and you can move on to a better one in the future.

CHAPTER 18

Matched

For true love is inexhaustible; the more you give, the more you have. And if you go to draw at the true fountainhead, the more water you draw, the more abundant is its flow.

-Antoine de Saint-Exupery

A funny thing happened on the journey towards completing this book.

I was working closely with an editor to help shape the manuscript. We spoke almost daily as she reviewed the book, making suggestions, and helping me clarify the stories and techniques of *Matched*.

One day, I realized I'd received no updates from her—no new suggestions, or requests for more information. I reached out but didn't hear back. It was as if she'd vanished.

Eventually, I discovered what had happened. While working her way through the book, she began to take the techniques and lessons to heart. She was single at the time, having broken up with a toxic boyfriend, and like so many of us, hoping to find that special someone. Using the ideas in *Matched,* she began to change her approach to dating. Within a short time, she'd found someone new.

That was why she'd disappeared. She'd found new love using my book!

Needless to say, I'd lost an editor, at least temporarily. She was caught up in the whirlwind of having found someone who she thought might last and started a new loving relationship with him.

But I'd found one more story and even more confidence that with the right approach, anyone can be *matched.* Within a short period of time, their love affair blossomed, and they are now engaged to be married.

Compromise, Don't Settle

Even if you haven't yet found your special someone, keep looking. *Don't settle!* Settling is selling yourself short and not being authentic.

Compromise, however, is something different. You cannot get *everything* you want in another person. You won't check every single box on your wish lists. Expecting this means you are too picky, unrealistic, or both. People are imperfect beings. There is no perfect man or woman out there. You certainly are not perfect either.

Instead, your goal is to find someone who meets the vast majority of your criteria—someone you can be your true self with, with whom you have great chemistry, and whose less-endearing qualities you are willing to compromise on. That means meeting *most* of your criteria. If you settle for less than most of what you want, you are robbing yourself of the opportunity to find a better match and a fulfilling long-term relationship.

A relationship will always require hard work, but if the other person is not even halfway there, don't invest too much. Your partner will not change *that* much. No one really changes at their core, and you cannot fix another person. Changing some *behaviors* and *habits* is possible if your partner is interested, but if your partner's values, characteristics, and behaviors over time do not fit with what you really want, move on.

If you settle now, you may gain temporary comfort but at the expense of your long-term happiness. Imagine how happy you would be with a partner who is supportive of you, who loves, respects, and adores you, and treats you well. Life is too short to waste or to end in regret. Don't waste time and energy in a low-quality match. You are better off alone.

Don't Get Discouraged

Treat dating as a learning and growth experience where you learn new things each time, including what not to do. Focus on improving with practice. Each time you "fail," recognize that it's not a failure, but a learning experience. Whether someone did not work out for *you* or you did not work out for *them*, you are now one step closer to finding the right match. It's much better to cut it off as a mismatch earlier in the relationship before you get hurt, and move on to your next partner quicker.

Every dating experience can lead to discovering something new about yourself. Each person coming into your life can teach you something. Even if you break up, ask yourself what you could have done better and how you can improve for your next partner. The secret to success in dating and in life is to be persistent and consistent. Don't give up. Finding the right match takes time.

**

So how did my own search for a dream relationship end? I am in a loving relationship now. I am hopeful and excited about the potential and the possibilities.

We are compatible in almost every way imaginable. He is loving, brilliant, authentic, supportive, honest, successful, fun, exciting, and makes me laugh like crazy. He sees me for who I really am. He recognizes that I am a powerful woman; better yet, he *loves* that about me and is attracted to it because he is a powerful man himself in a wonderful way that is charming and easy-going.

He loves that I can challenge him and push him to become a better man. We both enjoy our deep and intelligent conversations, how we laugh like crazy and have so much fun together. We have the best sexual chemistry and compatibility, and our combined presence and energy complement and uplift each other.

From the first texting session, I knew Allan was special. The conversation flowed with such ease that we did not realize that three hours had gone by in an instant. Every time we spoke, time seemed to vanish as we discovered each other. We completely lost all track of time, skipping the usual small talk and diving into deep and important topics like our values and beliefs. Losing all track of time and having the relationship just flow and grow naturally without effort are strong signs of a good match.

I could immediately tell that his psychological strength as a man, combined with his willingness to open up himself to me emotionally, was one of a kind. He couldn't have known at the time that this was one of the most important attributes to me in a partner.

I knew Allan was not interested in playing games, and I never had to question whether he was *really* into me or not. He texted me the morning right after our first phone conversation, and called just to hear my voice. Our text sessions and phone and video calls continued at a steady pace, and he quickly moved things forward to more in-person dates with the clear intention that he knew what he wanted and was unabashed about going after it. He had no fear of being perceived as needy or insecure by sending multiple texts daily and calling frequently. He simply communicated how he felt about me or when he wanted to see me or hear my voice.

We talk about everything, and we can laugh about everything, including ourselves. If there is a problem, we discuss it openly and immediately and do not let resentment build. We are very honest with each other and respect each other greatly. He is honest in everything he does and has never broken a promise to me or canceled at the last minute. He even rescheduled an important business meeting because it fell on my free afternoon, and he preferred to spend the time with me.

Our first date lasted four hours and felt like an instant. We kept talking over dinner until they closed the restaurant on us. We just did not want to say goodbye. Our second date also lasted hours and felt like an instant. I was surprised that he had not even kissed me on the first or second dates and instead just gave me hugs. When I asked him why, he said it was out of respect for me, because he was not sure whether I wanted him to, or whether I was seeing someone else. I told him that I was seeing someone else but broke it off right after our date felt right to me.

We progressed our relationship and talked and chatted on video and phone for hours on end, at any free minute we both had. On the third date, we finally kissed as soon as we saw each other (after he asked permission, of course). Our first kiss was magical, and sparks flew both ways that grew to an all-consuming fire. We made out for a few hours and became exclusive right after that.

Allan and I are building a loving relationship to last a lifetime. When he kisses or touches me, I just melt. I feel butterflies in my stomach even when he's not around. I miss him when he's away, and I have never felt such a deep connection and attraction to someone in my entire life. I feel a deep fire inside, and my passion is endless. I feel it in him, as well, especially in person, since he can't stop staring at me or touching me.

He is considerate, gentle, and loving—even though he is so manly and strong, he can crush most people with his fist! When he looks at me or smiles at me or touches me, I know that he is all in. He knows I am the best thing that has happened to him and that he will never find another woman like me. And I feel the same. He's a true *mensch*, a man of honor.

Allan always follows words with consistent actions. He pushes my boundaries without breaking them, and I push his. We grow together, willing to change. He brings out the best in me, and I bring out the best in him. He is romantic, caring, and loving—truly the best partner and lover I have ever had.

Every day is a new adventure with him, and he finds new ways to display his love for me and to delight me. He sees into me for who I really am, likes *all* of me, even my less appealing type-A qualities. For him, my ambition and drive are a bonus. He knows I am amazing and incredible and unique, the best woman he has ever met. He treats me in the best manner manifesting deep love, admiration, and respect that no man has ever treated me before at this level. He is my unicorn, *my* best man.

The Journey Ahead

The journey of discovery of both yourself and your partner is amazing. As long as you continue on this journey with your eyes wide open, aware of their behaviors, attitudes, how they treat you, and where your boundaries are, you will be on the right path.

While you can have relationship goals, set them like you set the sails on a boat. Act with good and clear intentions, and start your journey with the first action: setting your sails and pointing toward your destination. From there, let the water and wind carry you forward, and enjoy this amazing journey.

You may not reach the exact destination that you planned. The journey may be longer or shorter than you anticipate. There will be many different waves and currents on the sea. Life will always pull you in different directions, but you can still enjoy the journey.

Every relationship, even if it ends in a break-up, gets you one step closer to a better one. You will not have wasted your time and effort if you have a good time and enjoy the journey and all its amazing feelings and experiences. You never truly begin again, because you will always have learned about yourself and your partner, and what ultimately does and does not work for you.

On your journey, you will also improve the relationship you have with yourself as you will build your self-confidence and love for yourself. Enjoy the opportunity to become more honest, open, vulnerable, courageous, and authentic. Keep your lists and homework at hand for the moments you need reassurance. Let your true self shine.

Love

My definition of love is a version of Dr. Brené Brown's words: *a gift of love is an action or behavior of affection or kindness towards another person that comes from true connection and openness between two people who like, respect, and trust each other as their truest selves.*

Enjoy this beautiful journey of fun, laughter, amazing experiences, sex, and love. Love is not just a feeling; love requires action. It requires affection, kindness, and consideration toward another. Love is a *verb*. If someone says he loves me but acts in the opposite manner, I choose not to believe his words. In his book *Real Love,* Dr. Greg Baer says, "Real love is caring about the happiness of another person without any thought for what we might get for ourselves." I wholeheartedly agree. It's so uplifting for me to bring a smile to my love's face.

I know I deserve love, and I know I can give love. It is an endless resource and energy that you can renew each day. You deserve love, connection, and a wonderful relationship, so *believe it.* Set your intentions and actions towards love, and always remember to love yourself. Don't sell yourself short or settle for Mr. or Mrs. Right Now because it feels okay at the moment. If, at some point in the relationship, you discover that they are not the best match for *you,* break it off and keep looking for *your* best match based on *your* criteria.

I will not settle for anything less, and I hope I have empowered you to not settle, either. You *can* find your perfect match. Use the lessons of this book and continue your search with grit until you find it.

I wish you lots of love in your future,
Karen

ACKNOWLEDGMENTS

I didn't set out to write a relationship book. In fact, I started by making dating mistakes; I was anything *but* qualified to write a book. But as I became more "date smart," I began to keep notes on what was working and what wasn't. Eventually, those notes grew into a unique approach to dating, and I began to think about sharing what I had built with the world. But to turn my system into a book was a journey, and I have a few people to thank who were instrumental in the process.

Joe, you are a brilliant man with an inquisitive and intuitive mind. Thank you for encouraging me to tell my story and challenging me to share my system as a book that could empower others to date smarter for better results.

To my bestie Yelena, I owe you a huge debt of gratitude. You supported me in so many ways during my dating—listening, checking up on me, giving advice, and helping me interpret all the weird and wonderful things that happen in the world of dating. You were a voice of reason in a highly emotional and challenging arena where people play games and hurt others. Thankfully, you taught me a few tricks of my own, and a lot of your advice has found its way into this book.

Chris, thank you for challenging my paradigm by being the devil's advocate. Your observations were brilliant and gave me deep insights that helped me develop the male perspective.

To my first editor Laurie, many thanks for your honesty and for significantly improving the flow and readability of this book to help it reach a wider audience. I wish you continued relationship bliss.

Dan, my second editor, you are a magician with words, sentences and stories, thank you for helping me to get this book to its ultimate level. You helped me to push myself on many rewrites, and bring out the best in me and in my stories.

Hemant, you will always have my deep gratitude as the first man who treated me properly, with the utmost respect, care, sensitivity, and admiration. You set a high bar for other men, and that helped me to quickly weed out those who did not even come close. Love can truly transcend culture, upbringing, race, religion, and so much more—thank you for yours.

To all the men who have loved me along my dating and life journey, you gave me incredible gifts of love, joy, happiness, excitement, fun, appreciation, admiration, support, confidence, knowledge, and much more. I am grateful that our paths crossed and for all that you taught me about myself, relationships, human nature, and love.

To Allan, my best man, you have my eternal heartfelt gratitude, as you brought such delight, joy, fun, passion, and love to my life—you were both a new beginning and the happiest ending to this book.

RESOURCES

Qualities

This list may assist you in determining some of your personal qualities and characteristics that you may not have thought of otherwise. This was adapted from: Anderson, N. H. (1968). Likableness ratings of 555 personality-trait words. Journal of Social Psychology, 9, 272-279.

1. Sincere
2. Honest
3. Understanding
4. Loyal
5. Truthful
6. Trustworthy
7. Intelligent
8. Dependable
9. Open-Minded
10. Thoughtful
11. Wise
12. Considerate
13. Good-Natured
14. Reliable
15. Mature
16. Warm
17. Earnest
18. Kind
19. Friendly
20. Affectionate
21. Happy
22. Clean
23. Interesting
24. Unselfish
25. Good-Humored
26. Honorable
27. Humorous
28. Responsible
29. Cheerful
30. Trustful
31. Warm-Hearted
32. Broad-Minded
33. Gentle
34. Well-Spoken
35. Educated
36. Reasonable
37. Accepting
38. Likable
39. Trusting
40. Clever
41. Pleasant
42. Courteous
43. Quick-Witted
44. Tactful
45. Helpful
46. Appreciative
47. Imaginative
48. Outstanding
49. Self-Disciplined
50. Brilliant
51. Level-Headed
52. Polite
53. Original
54. Smart

55. Forgiving
56. Sharp-Witted
57. Well-Read
58. Ambitious
59. Bright
60. Respectful
61. Efficient
62. Good-Tempered
63. Grateful
64. Conscientious
65. Resourceful
66. Alert
67. Good
68. Witty
69. Affirming
70. Agreeable
71. Admirable
72. Patient
73. Talented
74. Perceptive
75. Spirited
76. Well-Mannered
77. Cooperative
78. Ethical
79. Intellectual
80. Versatile
81. Capable
82. Courageous
83. Constructive
84. Productive
85. Progressive
86. Individualistic
87. Observant
88. Ingenious
89. Lively
90. Neat
91. Punctual
92. Logical
93. Prompt
94. Accurate
95. Sensible
96. Creative
97. Self-Reliant
98. Tolerant
99. Amusing
100. Clean-Cut
101. Generous
102. Sympathetic
103. Energetic
104. High-Spirited
105. Self-Controlled
106. Accommodating
107. Active
108. Independent
109. Respectable
110. Inventive
111. Wholesome
112. Congenial
113. Cordial
114. Experienced
115. Attentive
116. Cultured
117. Frank
118. Purposeful
119. Decent
120. Diligent
121. Realist
122. Eager
123. Poised
124. Competent
125. Realistic
126. Amiable
127. Optimistic
128. Vigorous
129. Entertaining
130. Adventurous
131. Articulate
132. Composed
133. Relaxed
134. Romantic
135. Proficient
136. Rational
137. Skillful
138. Enterprising
139. Gracious
140. Able
141. Nice
142. Agreeable
143. Skilled
144. Curious
145. Modern
146. Charming
147. Sociable
148. Modest
149. Decisive
150. Humble
151. Tidy
152. Popular
153. Upright

154. Literary
155. Practical
156. Light-Hearted
157. Well-Bred
158. Refined
159. Self-Confident
160. Cool-Headed
161. Studious
162. Adventurous
163. Discreet
164. Informal
165. Thorough
166. Exuberant
167. Inquisitive
168. Easygoing
169. Outgoing
170. Self-Sufficient
171. Casual
172. Consistent
173. Moral
174. Self-Assured
175. Untiring
176. Hopeful
177. Calm
178. Strong-Minded
179. Positive
180. Confident
181. Artistic
182. Precise
183. Scientific
184. Orderly
185. Social
186. Direct
187. Careful
188. Candid
189. Comical
190. Obliging
191. Self-Critical
192. Fashionable
193. Religious
194. Soft-Hearted
195. Dignified
196. Philosophical
197. Idealistic
198. Soft-Spoken
199. Disciplined
200. Serious
201. Definite
202. Convincing
203. Persuasive
204. Obedient
205. Quick
206. Sophisticated
207. Thrifty
208. Sentimental
209. Objective
210. Nonconforming
211. Righteous
212. Fearless
213. Systematic
214. Subtle
215. Normal
216. Daring
217. Middleclass
218. Lucky
219. Proud
220. Sensitive
221. Moralistic
222. Talkative
223. Excited
224. Moderate
225. Satirical
226. Prudent
227. Reserved
228. Persistent
229. Meticulous
230. Unconventional
231. Deliberate
232. Painstaking
233. Bold
234. Suave
235. Cautious
236. Innocent
237. Inoffensive
238. Shrewd
239. Methodical
240. Nonchalant
241. Self-Contented
242. Perfectionist
243. Forward
244. Excitable
245. Outspoken
246. Prideful
247. Quiet
248. Impulsive
249. Aggressive
250. Changeable
251. Conservative
252. Shy

253. Hesitant
254. Unpredictable
255. Solemn
256. Blunt
257. Self-Righteous
258. Average
259. Discriminating
260. Emotional
261. Unlucky
262. Bashful
263. Self-Concerned
264. Authoritative
265. Lonesome
266. Restless
267. Choosy
268. Self-Possessed
269. Naive
270. Opportunist
271. Theatrical
272. Unsophisticated
273. Impressionable
274. Ordinary
275. Strict
276. Skeptical
277. Extravagant
278. Forceful
279. Cunning
280. Inexperienced
281. Unmethodical
282. Daredevil
283. Wordy
284. Daydreamer
285. Conventional

286. Materialistic
287. Self-Satisfied
288. Rebellious
289. Eccentric
290. Opinionated
291. Stern
292. Lonely
293. Dependent
294. Unsystematic
295. Self-Conscious
296. Undecided
297. Resigned
298. Anxious
299. Conforming
300. Critical
301. Conformist
302. Radical
303. Dissatisfied
304. Old-Fashioned
305. Meek
306. Frivolous
307. Discontented
308. Troubled
309. Irreligious
310. Silent
311. Tough
312. Graceful
313. Argumentative
314. Withdrawing
315. Forgetful
316. Inhibited
317. Unskilled
318. Crafty

319. Passive
320. Immodest
321. Unpopular
322. Timid
323. Temperamental
324. Gullible
325. Indecisive
326. Silly
327. Submissive
328. Preoccupied
329. Tense
330. Fearful
331. Unromantic
332. Absent-Minded
333. Impractical
334. Withdrawn
335. Sarcastic
336. Sad
337. Unemotional
338. Worrying
339. High-Strung
340. Unoriginal
341. Unpoised
342. Compulsive
343. Worrier
344. Demanding
345. Unhappy
346. Indifferent
347. Uncultured
348. Clumsy
349. Insecure
350. Assertive
351. Melancholy

352. Mediocre
353. Obstinate
354. Unhealthy
355. Headstrong
356. Nervous
357. Stubborn
358. Unimaginative
359. Unobservant
360. Inconsistent
361. Unpunctual
362. Industrious
363. Disturbed
364. Superstitious
365. Frustrated
366. Illogical
367. Rash
368. Unenthusiastic
369. Inaccurate
370. Jumpy
371. Possessive
372. Purposeless
373. Moody
374. Diplomatic
375. Insightful
376. Unwise
377. Oversensitive
378. Inefficient
379. Reckless
380. Pompous
381. Uncongenial
382. Untidy
383. Unaccommodating
384. Noisy
385. Squeamish
386. Cynical
387. Angry
388. Listless
389. Uninspiring
390. Intuitive
391. Domineering
392. Scolding
393. Depressed
394. Unobliging
395. Pessimistic
396. Attentive
397. Boisterous
398. Suspicious
399. Inattentive
400. Overconfident
401. Smug
402. Unsociable
403. Unfriendly
404. Wasteful
405. Fickle
406. Neglectful
407. Short-Tempered
408. Hot-Headed
409. Unsocial
410. Envious
411. Sly
412. Weak
413. Foolhardy
414. Immature
415. Dominating
416. Encouraging
417. Sloppy
418. Altruistic
419. Uncompromising
420. Hot-Tempered
421. Neurotic
422. Introverted
423. Extroverted
424. Resentful
425. Unruly
426. Effective
427. Messy
428. Analytical
429. Growth-Oriented
430. Frugal
431. Antisocial
432. Irritable
433. Stingy
434. Tactless
435. Careless
436. Foolish
437. Troublesome
438. Ungracious
439. Negligent
440. Wishy-Washy
441. Profane
442. Gloomy
443. Helpless
444. Disagreeable
445. Touchy
446. Irrational
447. Finicky
448. Disobedient
449. Complaining
450. Lifeless

451. Vain
452. Lazy
453. Unappreciative
454. Maladjusted
455. Aimless
456. Boastful
457. Dull
458. Gossipy
459. Genuine
460. Hypochondriac
461. Irritating
462. Petty
463. Shallow
464. Deceptive
465. Grouchy
466. Egotistical
467. Compassionate
468. Uncivil
469. Cold
470. Bossy
471. Unpleasing
472. Cowardly
473. Discourteous
474. Incompetent
475. Childish
476. Superficial
477. Ungrateful
478. Hard-Working
479. Balanced
480. Unfair
481. Irresponsible
482. Prejudiced
483. Bragging

484. Jealous
485. Unpleasant
486. Unreliable
487. Impolite
488. Crude
489. Nosey
490. Caring
491. Rude
492. Abusive
493. Distrustful
494. Intolerant
495. Flexible
496. Boring
497. Unethical
498. Unreasonable
499. Self-Centered
500. Snobbish
501. Unkindly
502. Ill-Mannered
503. Ill-Tempered
504. Hostile
505. Offensive
506. Belligerent
507. Annoying
508. Disrespectful
509. Easy-Going
510. Selfish
511. Narrow-Minded
512. Vulgar
513. Authentic
514. Comforting
515. Thoughtless
516. Communicative

517. Conceited
518. Greedy
519. Spiteful
520. Insulting
521. Insincere
522. Unkind
523. Untrustworthy
524. Deceitful
525. Dishonorable
526. Malicious
527. Obnoxious
528. Untruthful
529. Dishonest
530. Cruel
531. Mean
532. Phony
533. Liar

Values

The following is a list of over 200 personal values that may help you in determining who you are at your core and how you wish that your partner will be aligned with you. Taken from:

1. Acceptance
2. Accomplishment
3. Accountability
4. Accuracy
5. Achievement
6. Adaptability
7. Alertness
8. Altruism
9. Ambition
10. Amusement
11. Assertiveness
12. Attentive
13. Awareness
14. Balance
15. Beauty
16. Boldness
17. Bravery
18. Brilliance
19. Calm
20. Candor
21. Capable

22. Careful
23. Certainty
24. Challenge
25. Charity
26. Cleanliness
27. Clear
28. Clever
29. Comfort
30. Commitment
31. Common sense
32. Communication
33. Community
34. Compassion
35. Competence
36. Concentration
37. Confidence
38. Connection
39. Consciousness
40. Consistency
41. Contentment
42. Contribution

43. Control
44. Conviction
45. Cooperation
46. Courage
47. Courtesy
48. Creation
49. Creativity
50. Credibility
51. Curiosity
52. Decisive
53. Decisiveness
54. Dedication
55. Dependability
56. Determination
57. Development
58. Devotion
59. Dignity
60. Discipline
61. Discovery
62. Drive
63. Effectiveness

64. Efficiency
65. Empathy
66. Empower
67. Endurance
68. Energy
69. Enjoyment
70. Enthusiasm
71. Equality
72. Ethical
73. Excellence
74. Experience
75. Exploration
76. Expressive
77. Fairness
78. Family
79. Famous
80. Fearless
81. Feelings
82. Ferocious
83. Fidelity
84. Focus
85. Foresight
86. Fortitude
87. Freedom
88. Friendship
89. Fun
90. Generosity
91. Genius
92. Giving
93. Goodness
94. Grace
95. Gratitude
96. Greatness
97. Growth
98. Happiness

99. Hard work
100. Harmony
101. Health
102. Honesty
103. Honor
104. Hope
105. Humility
106. Humor
107. Imagination
108. Improvement
109. Independence
110. Individuality
111. Innovation
112. Inquisitive
113. Insightful
114. Inspiring
115. Integrity
116. Intelligence
117. Intensity
118. Intuitive
119. Joy
120. Justice
121. Kindness
122. Knowledge
123. Lawful
124. Leadership
125. Learning
126. Liberty
127. Logic
128. Love
129. Loyalty
130. Mastery
131. Maturity
132. Meaning
133. Moderation

134. Motivation
135. Openness
136. Optimism
137. Order
138. Organization
139. Originality
140. Passion
141. Patience
142. Peace
143. Performance
144. Persistence
145. Playfulness
146. Poise
147. Potential
148. Power
149. Present
150. Productivity
151. Professionalism
152. Prosperity
153. Purpose
154. Quality
155. Realistic
156. Reason
157. Recognition
158. Recreation
159. Reflective
160. Respect
161. Responsibility
162. Restraint
163. Results-oriented
164. Reverence
165. Rigor
166. Risk
167. Satisfaction
168. Security

169. Self-reliance
170. Selfless
171. Sensitivity
172. Serenity
173. Service
174. Sharing
175. Significance
176. Silence
177. Simplicity
178. Sincerity
179. Skill
180. Skillfulness
181. Smart
182. Solitude
183. Spirit
184. Spirituality
185. Spontaneous
186. Stability
187. Status
188. Stewardship
189. Strength
190. Structure
191. Success
192. Support
193. Surprise
194. Sustainability
195. Talent
196. Teamwork
197. Temperance
198. Thankful
199. Thorough
200. Thoughtful
201. Timeliness
202. Tolerance
203. Toughness

204. Traditional
205. Tranquility
206. Transparency
207. Trust
208. Trustworthy
209. Truth
210. Understanding
211. Uniqueness
212. Unity
213. Valor
214. Victory
215. Vigor
216. Vision
217. Vitality
218. Wealth
219. Welcoming
220. Winning
221. Wisdom
222. Wonder

36 QUESTIONS THAT LEAD TO LOVE

From: https://www.nytimes.com/2015/01/09/style/no-37-big-wedding-or-small.html

Set I

1. Given the choice of anyone in the world, whom would you want as a dinner guest?

2. Would you like to be famous? In what way?

3. Before making a telephone call, do you ever rehearse what you are going to say? Why?

4. What would constitute a "perfect" day for you?

5. When did you last sing to yourself? To someone else?

6. If you were able to live to the age of 90 and retain either the mind or body of a 30-year-old for the last 60 years of your life, which would you want?

7. Do you have a secret hunch about how you will die?

8. Name three things you and your partner appear to have in common.

9. For what in your life do you feel most grateful?

10. If you could change anything about the way you were raised, what would it be?

11. Take four minutes and tell your partner your life story in as much detail as possible.

12. If you could wake up tomorrow having gained any one quality or ability, what would it be?

Set II

12. If a crystal ball could tell you the truth about yourself, your life, the future or anything else, what would you want to know?

13. Is there something that you've dreamed of doing for a long time? Why haven't you done it?

14. What is the greatest accomplishment of your life?

15. What do you value most in a friendship?

16. What is your most treasured memory?

17. What is your most terrible memory?

18. If you knew that in one year you would die suddenly, would you change anything about the way you are now living? Why?

19. What does friendship mean to you?

20. What roles do love and affection play in your life?

21. Alternate sharing something you consider a positive characteristic of your partner. Share a total of five items.

22. How close and warm is your family? Do you feel your childhood was happier than most other people's?

23. How do you feel about your relationship with your mother?

Set III

24. Make three true "we" statements each. For instance, "We are both in this room feeling ... "

25. Complete this sentence: "I wish I had someone with whom I could share ... "

26. If you were going to become a close friend with your partner, please share what would be important for him or her to know.

27. Tell your partner what you like about them; be very honest this time, saying things that you might not say to someone you've just met.

28. Share with your partner an embarrassing moment in your life.

29. When did you last cry in front of another person? By yourself?

30. Tell your partner something that you like about them already.

31. What, if anything, is too serious to be joked about?

32. If you were to die this evening with no opportunity to communicate with anyone, what would you most regret not having told someone? Why haven't you told them yet?

33. Your house, containing everything you own, catches fire. After saving your loved ones and pets, you have time to safely make a final dash to save any one item. What would it be? Why?

34. Of all the people in your family, whose death would you find most disturbing? Why?

35. Share a personal problem and ask your partner's advice on how he or she might handle it. Also, ask your partner to reflect back to you how you seem to be feeling about the problem you have chosen.

Made in the USA
Columbia, SC
28 January 2021